# Great Escapes
## Italy

*Edited & compiled by* Angelika Taschen    *Texts by* Christiane Reiter

# Great Escapes
## Italy

TASCHEN

# Contents   Inhalt   Sommaire

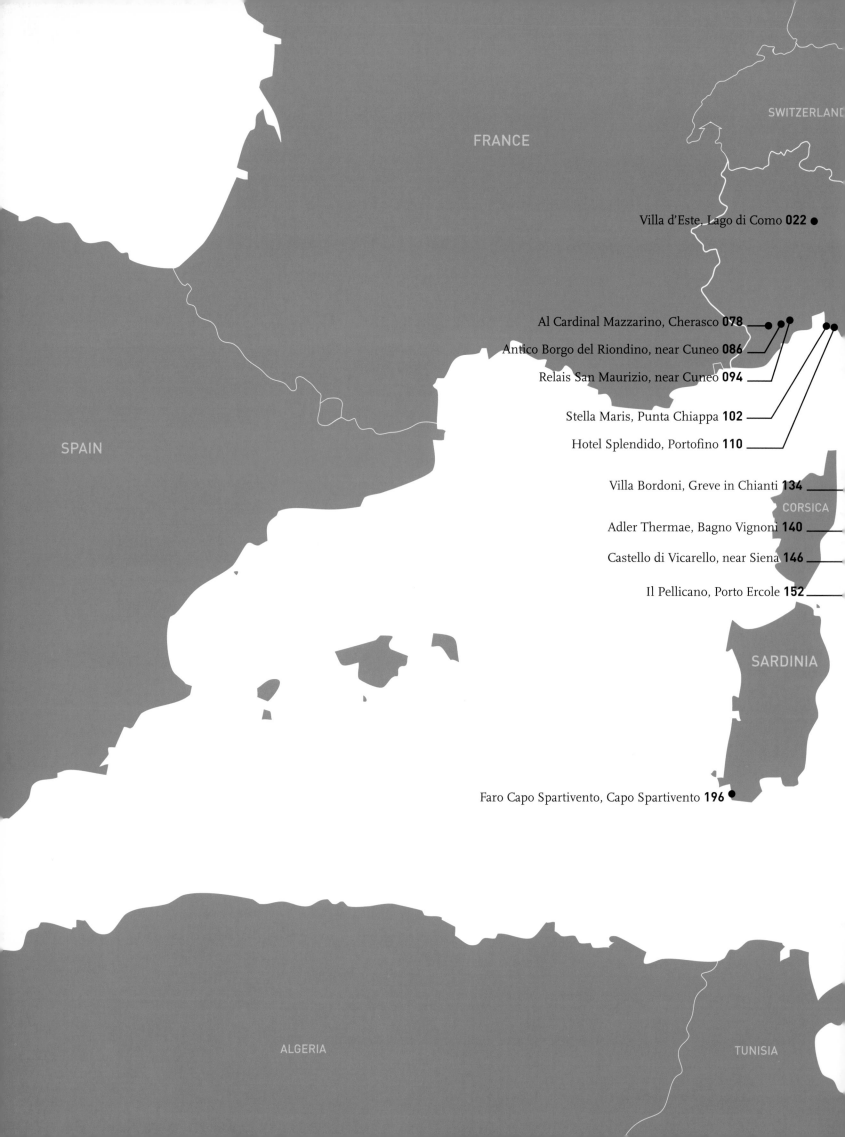

**008** Vigilius Mountain Resort, Lana

**016** Pension Briol, Barbiano-Tre Chiese

**030** Villa Feltrinelli, Lago di Garda

**038** Villa Amistà, near Verona

**046** Locanda Cipriani, Torcello

**062** Hotel Flora, Venezia

**070** Villa Pisani, near Padova

**118** Torre di Bellosguardo, Firenze

**160** Palazzo Terranova, near Perugia

**170** Locanda del Gallo, Gubbio

**178** Casa San Ruffino, Montegiorgio

**186** Sextantio S. Stefano di Sessanio, near L'Aquila

**236** Sextantio Le Grotte della Civita, Matera

**244** La Sommità, Ostuni

Mezzatorre, Ischia **202**

Il San Pietro, Positano **208**

**252** Villa Cenci, Cisternino

Hotel Palumbo, Ravello **212**

Villa Cimbrone, Ravello **220**

**262** Relais Histó S. Pietro sul Mar Piccolo, Taranto

**270** Convento di Santa Maria di Costantinopoli, Marittima di Diso

Palazzo Belmonte, Salerno **230**

**284** Capofaro, Salina

**292** Il Gattopardo, Isola di Lampedusa

# Perfect Peace
Vigilius Mountain Resort, Lana

# Vigilius Mountain Resort, Lana

**Perfect Peace**

Seven minutes is all you need to travel to a different world. That's how long the cable car takes to glide from Lana in the valley to a height of 4,921 feet – to the Vigiljoch, where there are no cars, no traffic noise, no open-plan offices and no supermarkets. Those who escape here from everyday cares can enjoy a view of the Tyrolean peaks, breathe air that seems to tingle with the aroma of larch forests and walk over meadows where gentians flower. Back in the mists of time a pious giant is said to have lived in this mountain idyll and built a church. At the start of the third millennium Matteo Thun took his cue from these first architectural traces and designed the Vigilius Mountain Resort. Born in Alto Adige (South Tyrol) himself, Thun wanted to give his homeland a hotel whose architecture took up and evolved the forms of nature, a hotel that combined tradition with modern standards. The building lies on the slope like a huge tree trunk, made from wood, stone and glass. It was thought out down to the last detail: the flat roof was greened thanks to a layer of soil, and in the simply designed rooms a heated earthen wall separates the living area from the bathroom – a wonderful source of warmth, especially in winter! And a natural source of water – a spring – supplies the spa, where the simple bodycare products are real treasures: a mountain herbal massage or a Tyrolean hay bath bring guests even closer to heaven than they already are at 4,921 feet.
**Book to pack: "The Cantos" by Ezra Pound.**

| | |
|---|---|
| **Vigilius Mountain Resort** | |
| Vigiljoch Mountain | |
| 39011 Lana | |
| Italy | |
| Tel. +39 0473 556 600 | |
| Fax +39 0473 556 699 | |
| info@vigilius.it | |
| www.vigilius.it | |
| **Open all year round** | |

| | |
|---|---|
| DIRECTIONS | 15 miles north of Bolzano. The cable car operates daily every 30 min from 8 am to 7.30 pm in the summer. |
| RATES | Rooms from 190 €, suites from 565 €, including breakfast. |
| ROOMS | 35 rooms and 6 suites. |
| FOOD | Down-to-earth Tyrolean food in "Stube Ida", light natural cuisine with absolutely fresh herbs in the restaurant "1500". |
| HISTORY | The resort opened in September 2003. |
| X-FACTOR | Outstanding personal trainers for indoor and outdoor sports. |

## In aller Ruhe

Die Reise in eine andere Welt dauert nur sieben Minuten. So lange braucht die Seilbahn, um von der Talstation in Lana auf 1.500 Meter Höhe zu schweben – aufs Vigiljoch, wo es keine Autos und keinen Straßenlärm gibt, keine Großraumbüros und keine Supermärkte. Weit weg vom Alltag genießt man hier stattdessen den Blick auf Südtirols Gipfel, atmet fast prickelnde Luft mit Lärchenwaldaroma und läuft über Wiesen, auf denen der Enzian blüht. In dieser Bergidylle soll vor Urzeiten ein frommer Riese gelebt und eine Kirche gebaut haben – Anfang des dritten Jahrtausends folgte Matteo Thun diesen ersten architektonischen Spuren und entwarf das Vigilius Mountain Resort. Selbst in Südtirol geboren, wollte Thun seiner Heimat ein Hotel geben, dessen Architektur die Formen der Natur aufgreift und fortschreibt und das alte Traditionen mit modernen Ansprüchen verbindet. Wie ein mächtiger Baumstamm liegt das Gebäude am Hang – aus Holz, Stein sowie Glas konstruiert und mit durchdachten Details versehen: So wurde das Flachdach dank einer Humusschicht begrünt, und in den schnörkellos designten Zimmern werden Wohnbereich und Bad durch eine beheizte Lehmwand getrennt – vor allem im Winter eine herrliche Wärmequelle! Eine weitere Wasser-Quelle speist das Spa, in dem sich schlichte Pflegeprodukte als wahre Schätze erweisen: Eine Bergkräuter-Massage oder ein Südtiroler Heubad bringen den Gast dem Himmel noch näher, als man in 1.500 Metern Höhe ohnehin schon ist.
**Buchtipp: »Der Himmel über Meran« von Joseph Zoderer.**

## En toute quiétude

Il suffit de sept minutes pour arriver dans un autre monde, le temps nécessaire à la télécabine partie de la station de la vallée à Lana pour rejoindre le Vigiljoch à 1500 mètres d'altitude, là où il n'y a ni voitures ni bruits de circulation, ni bureaux paysagers ni supermarchés. Loin du quotidien, on jouit ici de la vue sur les sommets du Tyrol du Sud, on respire un air vivifiant qui embaume le mélèze et on foule des prairies où fleurit la gentiane. On raconte qu'un géant très croyant aurait vécu, il y a bien longtemps, dans cette région idyllique et qu'il aurait construit une église – Matteo Thun a suivi son exemple en concevant au début du troisième millénaire le Vigilius Mountain Resort. Natif du Tyrol du Sud, Thun voulait doter sa région d'un hôtel dont l'architecture reprendrait les formes de la nature et marierait les traditions anciennes et les exigences modernes. Tel un énorme tronc d'arbre, le bâtiment, construit en bois, en pierre et en verre et doté de détails sophistiqués, repose sur le flanc de la montagne. Le toit plat a ainsi été recouvert d'une couche d'humus pour le végétaliser et, dans les chambres au décor sobre, un mur en argile chauffé sépare la salle de bains et la partie séjour – rayonnant d'une sublime chaleur en hiver. Nature encore – de l'eau de source énergisante alimente le spa dans lequel des produits de soin tout simples s'avèrent très précieux : un massage aux plantes des montagnes ou un bain de foin sud-tyrolien nous emmène au septième ciel.
**Livre à emporter : « L'Hiver tyrolien » d'Elisabeth Demaison.**

| | | |
|---|---|---|
| ANREISE | 25 km nördlich von Bozen gelegen. Die Seilbahn fährt im Sommer täglich von 8–19:30 Uhr im 30-min-Takt. | |
| PREISE | Zimmer ab 190 €, Suite ab 565 €, inklusive Frühstück. | |
| ZIMMER | 35 Zimmer und 6 Suiten. | |
| KÜCHE | Bodenständiges aus Südtirol serviert die »Stube Ida«, im Restaurant »1500« gibt es leichte naturbelassene Menüs mit ganz frischen Kräutern. | |
| GESCHICHTE | Das Resort eröffnete im September 2003. | |
| X-FAKTOR | Die ausgezeichneten Personal Trainer für Indoor- und Outdoor-Sport. | |

| | |
|---|---|
| ACCÈS | Situé à 25 km au nord de Bolzano. La télécabine circule tous les jours de 8h à 19h30 et passe toutes les 30 min en été. |
| PRIX | Chambre à partir de 190 €, suite à partir de 565 €, petit-déjeuner inclus. |
| CHAMBRES | 35 chambres et 6 suites. |
| RESTAURATION | La « Stube Ida » vous réserve des spécialités rustiques du Tyrol du Sud, le restaurant « 1500 » sert une cuisine naturelle aux herbes, toute de légèreté. |
| HISTOIRE | Le Resort a ouvert ses portes en septembre 2003. |
| LES « PLUS » | Le remarquable coaching sportif à l'intérieur et l'extérieur. |

# Holidays from Grandmother's
Pension Briol, Barbiano-Tre Chiese

# Pension Briol, Barbiano-Tre Chiese

**Holidays from Grandmother's Days**

A high-carat ring, a beautiful dress or fine porcelain for special occasions – the classic gifts from a husband to his wife after the birth of their child were not what Johanna Settari dreamed of. The wish that she expressed while still in childbed was more unusual: a plot of land "on the mountain" was what she wanted, a property above the Eisack Valley in South Tyrol (Alto Adige), the homeland that she loved above all else. And as Johanna was married to a wealthy merchant from Bolzano, who made her wish come true for every child, and as she bore 14 girls and a boy, she eventually owned a considerable amount of land. The extended family enjoyed wonderful summers here, and soon had the company of tourists: guests who took a break from their everyday routine in Pension Briol, which was designed in 1928 by the artist Hubert Lanzinger, Johanna's son-in-law. In the plain Bauhaus style he produced a complete work of art in which every detail is both beautiful and functional, and harmonises ideally with the whole. To this day these surroundings have remained unchanged. The rooms are fitted with larch wood and have no curtains in order to keep the unobstructed view of the Dolomites. Guests use the original washbasins and are treated to specialities from the Settaris' old recipe book. The pension is run with heart and soul by Johanna's great-granddaughter: like all the properties "on the mountain", the house has stayed in family ownership, which was a further wish of the resolute lady who founded it. **Book to pack: "Klausen" by Andreas Maier, translation by Kenneth Northcutt.**

**Pension Briol**
39040 Barbiano – Tre Chiese
Val d'Isarco
Italy
Tel./Fax +39 0471 650 125
info@briol.it
www.briol.it
**Open from the end of April/beginning of May (as soon as the snow melts) to the middle of October**

| | |
|---|---|
| DIRECTIONS | 15 miles north of Bolzano at an altitude of 4,300 feet, accessible only on foot or by jeep taxi. |
| RATES | Rooms from 72 €, including half board. |
| ROOMS | 13 rooms (with two shared bathrooms) in the guesthouse, 4 rooms in the nearby annexe. |
| FOOD | Recipes derive from an aunt of the present owner who learned her trade in high-class households in Rome and Paris. |
| HISTORY | The pension was originally a mountain shelter built in 1898. |
| X-FACTOR | The oval pool with spring water and a view of the sunrise. |

## Urlaub wie zu Urgroßmutters Zeiten

Ein hochkarätiger Ring, ein traumhaftes Kleid oder feines Sonntagsporzellan – mit den Klassikern, die Ehemänner ihren Frauen nach der Geburt eines Babys schenken, konnte man Johanna Settari nicht begeistern. Sie äußerte vom Wochenbett aus einen ungewöhnlicheren Wunsch: Ein Stück Land »am Berg« wollte sie gerne haben; ein Grundstück oberhalb des Eisacktals – ihrer Südtiroler Heimat, die sie über alles liebte. Und da Johanna mit einem wohlhabenden Kaufmann aus Bozen verheiratet war, der ihr diesen Wunsch bei allen Kindern erfüllte und sie 14 Mädchen sowie einen Jungen zur Welt brachte, gehörte ihr schließlich ein sehr ansehnliches Areal. Hier verbrachte die Großfamilie herrliche Sommer – und bekam bald Gesellschaft von Touristen: Die Besucher nahmen ihre Auszeit vom Alltag in der Pension Briol, die Johannas Schwiegersohn, der Künstler Hubert Lanzinger, 1928 gestaltet hatte – im schnörkellosen Bauhaus-Stil und als Gesamtkunstwerk, in dem alle Details so schön wie funktional und ideal aufeinander abgestimmt sind. Bis heute wurde das Ambiente nicht verändert. Man wohnt in Zimmern, die mit Lärchenholz ausgestattet sind und zugunsten eines freien Dolomitenblicks auf Vorhänge verzichten, benutzt die originalen Waschschüsseln und schwelgt in Spezialitäten aus dem alten Rezeptbuch der Settaris. Mit viel Herz geführt wird die Pension von Johannas Urenkelin, denn das Haus ist wie alle Grundstücke »am Berg« stets im Besitz der Familie geblieben – auch dies war einst der Wunsch der resoluten Dame.

**Buchtipp: »Klausen« von Andreas Maier.**

## Des vacances comme chez grand-maman

Une bague précieuse, une robe de rêve ou de la porcelaine fine – ce que les maris offrent à leur épouse après la naissance d'un enfant n'éveillait pas l'enthousiasme de Johanna Settari qui, à peine relevée de couches, exprima un souhait inhabituel : elle désirait un terrain sur la montagne, au-dessus de la vallée de l'Isarco, sa patrie sud-tyrolienne qu'elle aimait plus que tout. Mariée à un riche marchand de Bolzano qui ne songeait qu'à la satisfaire, Johanna mit au monde quatorze filles et un garçon, ce qui fait que, finalement, elle se retrouva propriétaire d'un domaine de taille respectable. La famille passait ici des étés magnifiques – et bientôt elle ne fut plus la seule à profiter de la beauté des paysages. Les touristes venaient se détendre à la pension Briol que le gendre de Johanna, l'artiste Hubert Lanzinger, avait meublée et décorée en 1928 dans un style Bauhaus dépouillé, créant une œuvre d'art totale dont tous les détails sont aussi beaux que fonctionnels et s'harmonisent parfaitement. L'ambiance n'a pas changé. On loge dans des chambres parquetées de bois d'épicéa et sans rideaux, ce qui permet d'admirer les Dolomites dans toute leur splendeur ; on utilise les cuvettes d'origine et on savoure les spécialités cuisinées d'après le vieux livre de recettes des Settari. La pension est dirigée avec chaleur par l'arrière-petite-fille de Johanna, car la maison et tous les terrains sont restés en possession de la famille ainsi que l'avait imposé l'énergique ancêtre.

**Livre à emporter : « Les Gens de Chiusa » d'Andreas Maier.**

| | | | | |
|---|---|---|---|---|
| ANREISE | 25 km nördlich von Bozen auf 1.310 m Höhe gelegen und nur zu Fuß oder mit dem Jeep-Taxi erreichbar. | | ACCÈS | A 25 km au nord de Bolzano et à 1310 m d'altitude ; à pied ou en taxi-jeep. |
| PREISE | Zimmer ab 72 €, inklusive Halbpension. | | PRIX | Chambre à partir de 72 €, demi-pension incluse. |
| ZIMMER | 13 Zimmer (mit 2 Gemeinschaftsbädern) in der Pension, 4 Zimmer in der nahen Dependance. | | CHAMBRES | 13 chambres (avec deux salles de bains communes) dans la pension, 4 chambres dans la dépendance toute proche. |
| KÜCHE | Die Rezepte gehen auf eine Tante der heutigen Besitzerin zurück, die einst in noblen Haushalten in Rom und Paris lernte. | | RESTAURATION | La propriétaire actuelle utilise les recettes d'une tante qui fut formée autrefois dans de nobles maisons à Paris et à Rome. |
| GESCHICHTE | Die Pension entstand aus einem 1898 errichteten Schutzhaus. | | HISTOIRE | A l'origine, un gîte construit en 1898. |
| X-FAKTOR | Der ovale Pool mit Quellwasser und Blick in den Sonnenaufgang. | | LES « PLUS » | La piscine ovale avec son eau de source et sa vue sur le soleil levant. |

# A Lakeside Jewel
Villa d'Este, Lago di Como

# Villa d'Este, Lago di Como

**A Lakeside Jewel**

They were cardinals, kings and artists, rich and refined, extravagant and eccentric, and consumed with a passion for Lago di Como, one of Italy's most romantic lakes: they were the owners of Villa d'Este. From the mid-16th to the mid-19th century this noble estate belonged to, among others, the Italian Cardinal Tolomeo Gallio, the ballerina Vittoria Peluso, who performed her pirouettes on the stage of La Scala in Milan, Domenico Pino, a Napoleonic general who played war games on the shores of the lake with his cadets, and Caroline of Brunswick, who took refuge here from her unhappy marriage to George IV of England. The memory of their glamour and the opulent charm of the Old World live on in Villa d'Este, which is today one of the most luxurious hotels in Italy. All rooms are furnished with antiques, rustling silk from nearby Como and original works of art, and no two rooms are alike. Guests reside particularly stylishly in the Villa Regina wing, a trompe l'œil masterpiece. Those who are unable to book one of the coveted rooms with a balcony delight in the lake view from the floating pool deck and from the terrace at dinner. And a stroll through the perfectly manicured park is a chance to see faces known from Hollywood films: many of today's guests at Villa d'Este are no less famous than its owners of old.

**Book to pack: "The Charterhouse of Parma" by Stendhal.**

| | |
|---|---|
| **Villa d'Este** | |
| Via Regina 40 | |
| 22012 Cernobbio | |
| Italy | |
| Tel. +39 031 3481 | |
| Fax +39 031 348 844 | |
| info@villadeste.it | |
| www.villadeste.it | |
| **Open from the beginning of March to the middle of November** | |

| | |
|---|---|
| DIRECTIONS | At the south end of Lago di Como, 21 miles from Lugano Airport, 40 miles from Milan's Malpensa Airport. |
| RATES | Rooms from 415 €, including breakfast. |
| ROOMS | 125 rooms in Villa Cardinale, 27 rooms in Villa Regina and two private villas. |
| FOOD | "Veranda" is famous for its irresistible risotto, the "Grill" serves regional specialities. |
| HISTORY | Villa d'Este was built in 1568 by Pellegrino Pellegrini and has been a hotel since 1873. |
| X-FACTOR | The chic spa with its Zen atmosphere. |

### Ein Schmuckstück am See

Sie waren Kardinäle, Könige und Künstler, reich und raffiniert, extravagant und exzentrisch – und voller Leidenschaft
für den Comer See, der zu den romantischsten Seen Italiens
gehört: die Besitzer der Villa d'Este. Zwischen Mitte des
16. und Mitte des 19. Jahrhunderts gehörte das noble
Anwesen unter anderem dem italienischen Kardinal Tolomeo
Gallio, der Ballerina Vittoria Peluso, die auf der Bühne
der Mailänder Scala ihre Pirouetten drehte, dem General
Napoleons, Domenico Pino, der mit seinen Kadetten auf
dem Ufergrundstück Krieg spielte, sowie Caroline von
Braunschweig-Wolfenbüttel, die hier Zuflucht vor ihrer
unglücklichen Ehe mit Georg IV. von Großbritannien suchte.
Die Erinnerung an diese schillernden Persönlichkeiten und
der opulente Charme der Alten Welt sind in der Villa d'Este
– heute eines der luxuriösesten Hotels des Landes – noch
immer lebendig. Alle Zimmer wurden mit Antiquitäten,
knisternder Seide aus dem nahen Como sowie originaler
Kunst ausgestattet, und kein Raum gleicht dem anderen
– besonders schön wohnt man im Flügel Villa Regina,
einem Meisterwerk des Trompe-l'œil. Wer keines der be-
gehrten Zimmer mit Balkon bekommen kann, bewundert
den See vom schwimmenden Pooldeck aus und beim
Dinner auf der Terrasse. Und beim Spaziergang durch den
perfekt gestalteten Park kann man durchaus auf Gesichter
treffen, die man aus Hollywood-Filmen kennt – viele heutige
Gäste der Villa d'Este sind ebenso berühmt wie ihre einstigen Eigentümer.

**Buchtipp: »Die Kartause von Parma« von Stendhal.**

### Le joyau du lac

Princes de l'Eglise, monarques, artistes, personnages riches
et raffinés, extravagants et excentriques – les propriétaires
de la Villa d'Este aimaient tous passionnément le lac de
Côme, l'un des lacs les plus romantiques d'Italie. Entre le
milieu du XVIe et le milieu du XIXe siècle, le noble domaine
appartint, entre autres, au cardinal italien Tolomeo Gallio, à la
ballerine Vittoria Peluso qui évoluait sur la scène de la Scala
de Milan, à Domenico Pino, un général de Napoléon, qui
jouait à la guerre avec ses soldats sur les berges du lac, ainsi
qu'à Caroline de Brunswick qui tenta ici d'échapper à son
mariage malheureux avec George IV d'Angleterre. Le souvenir
de ces personnages hauts en couleur et le charme du Vieux
Monde sont encore bien vivants à la Villa d'Este, devenue l'un
des hôtels les plus luxueux du pays. Toutes les chambres sont
meublées et décorées d'antiquités, de soieries froufroutantes
originaires de Côme ainsi que d'œuvres d'art originales, et
aucune pièce n'est semblable à l'autre. L'aile Villa Regina
un chef-d'œuvre du trompe-l'œil, est particulièrement intéressante. Celui qui n'a pas la chance de séjourner dans une
des chambres avec balcon très convoitées admirera le lac
de la piscine flottante ou de la terrasse en dînant. Et les
promenades dans le superbe parc réservent des surprises :
on peut y rencontrer des stars de Hollywood – nombre des
clients actuels de la Villa d'Este sont aussi célèbres que ses
anciens propriétaires.

**Livre à emporter : « La Chartreuse de Parme » de Stendhal.**

| | | | | |
|---|---|---|---|---|
| ANREISE | Im Süden des Comer Sees gelegen, 35 km vom Flughafen Lugano, 65 km von Mailand-Malpensa entfernt. | ACCÈS | Situé au sud du lac de Côme, à 35 km de l'aéroport de Lugano, à 65 km de celui de Milan-Malpensa. |
| PREISE | Zimmer ab 415 €, inklusive Frühstück. | PRIX | Chambre à partir de 415 €, petit-déjeuner inclus. |
| ZIMMER | 125 Zimmer in der Villa Cardinale, 27 Zimmer in der Villa Regina und 2 private Villen. | CHAMBRES | 125 chambres dans la Villa Cardinale, 27 chambres dans la Villa Regina et deux villas privées. |
| KÜCHE | Das »Veranda« ist für unwiderstehlichen Risotto berühmt, der »Grill« serviert Spezialitäten der Region. | RESTAURATION | La « Veranda » est célèbre pour son irrésistible risotto, le « Grill » sert des spécialités régionales. |
| GESCHICHTE | Die Villa d'Este wurde 1568 von Pellegrino Pellegrini erbaut und ist seit 1873 ein Hotel. | HISTOIRE | Construite en 1568 par Pellegrino Pellegrini, la Villa d'Este est un hôtel depuis 1873. |
| X-FAKTOR | Das schicke Spa mit Zen-Atmosphäre. | LES « PLUS » | Le spa élégant et son atmosphère zen. |

# History and Grandezza
Villa Feltrinelli, Lago di Garda

# Villa Feltrinelli, Lago di Garda

**History and Grandezza**

A palazzo in "Stile Liberty" (Italian Art Nouveau), the scent of lemon and olive trees in the garden and Lago di Garda shining right at the door. That ought to be paradise. But Benito Mussolini took little pleasure in the magic of Villa Feltrinelli when he lived there from October 1943 to April 1945. It was not just that Hitler's generals had downgraded the once-powerful Duce to be head of a puppet regime. Mussolini hated water and thus the lake too, and had to adhere to an insipid diet as a result of stomach trouble and divide his private life between his wife and his mistress. Fortunately this kind of trouble, political or otherwise, has no place today – Villa Feltrinelli, originally built as the summer residence of the timber and publishing dynasty of the same name, has been converted into a hotel that strikes a perfect balance between luxurious elegance and a relaxed family atmosphere. With a feeling for history, architecture and art Babey Moulton Jue & Booth have restored the house and furnished it with the finest antiques. Venetian mirrors, tall fireplaces and lamps of mouth-blown glass adorn the rooms, seven of which even have ceiling frescoes by the Lieti brothers from the 1890s. Vintage editions of "National Geographic" are in the library and at the bar drinks are served in 1950s glasses. In the evenings guests indulge in Italian cuisine of such refinement that a Michelin star twinkles above it – to be sure, the days of Mussolini and his diet are over once and for all.

**Book to pack: "Twilight in Italy" by D. H. Lawrence.**

**Grand Hotel a Villa Feltrinelli**
Via Rimembranza 38–40
25084 Gargnano
Italy
Tel. +39 0365 798 000
Fax +39 0365 798 001
booking@villafeltrinelli.com
www.villafeltrinelli.com
**Open from the middle of April
to the middle of October**

| | |
|---|---|
| DIRECTIONS | On the west bank of Lago di Garda, 55 miles from Verona Airport. |
| RATES | Rooms from 900 €, including breakfast (minimum stay 2 nights). |
| ROOMS | 21 rooms and suites. |
| FOOD | The Venetian-inspired "The Pergola" has even more atmosphere than "The Dining Room". |
| HISTORY | The villa was built in 1892 by Alberico Barbiano di Belgioioso and bought in 1997 by the US hotelier Bob Burns. It has been a hotel since 2001. |
| X-FACTOR | Musical soirées around the Bösendorfer grand piano in the salon. |

## Geschichte und Grandezza

Ein Palazzo im italienischen Liberty-Stil, duftende Zitronen- und Olivenbäume im Garten und den glitzernden Gardasee direkt vor der Tür – ein Paradies, sollte man meinen. Doch Benito Mussolini hatte wenig vom Zauber der Villa Feltrinelli, als er von Oktober 1943 bis April 1945 hier lebte. Nicht nur, dass Hitlers Generäle den einst so mächtigen Duce zum Kopf eines Marionettenregimes degradierten – Mussolini hasste zu allem Überfluss das Wasser und damit den See, musste wegen Magenbeschwerden eine fade Diät halten und sein Privatleben zwischen Frau und Geliebter teilen. Solche (politischen) Unruhen spielen heute glücklicherweise keine Rolle mehr – die Villa Feltrinelli, einst als Sommersitz der gleichnamigen Holz- und Verlegerdynastie erbaut, wurde in ein Hotel verwandelt, das perfekt zwischen luxuriöser Eleganz und entspannt-familiärer Atmosphäre balanciert. Mit viel Sinn für Geschichte, Architektur und Kunst haben Babey Moulton Jue & Booth das Haus restauriert und mit den schönsten Antiquitäten ausgestattet. Venezianische Spiegel, hohe Kamine und mundgeblasene Glaslampen schmücken die Räume (sieben Zimmer besitzen sogar Deckenfresken der Brüder Lieti aus den 1890ern), in der Bibliothek liegen Vintage-Ausgaben des »National Geographic«, und an der Bar werden die Drinks in Gläsern aus den 1950ern serviert. Abends lässt man sich mit italienischer Küche verwöhnen, die so fein ist, dass über ihr ein Michelin-Stern strahlt – ja, Mussolini und seine Diät gehören definitiv der Vergangenheit an.

**Buchtipp: »Italienische Dämmerung« von D. H. Lawrence.**

## Vivre l'utopie

Un palais dans le style Liberty italien, des oliviers et des citronniers odorants dans les jardins et les eaux scintillantes du lac de Garde au pied de la porte – le paradis direz-vous. Benito Mussolini, qui vécut à la Villa Feltrinelli d'octobre 1943 à avril 1945, avait sûrement un autre avis sur la question. Non seulement les généraux de Hitler avaient mis le Duce autrefois si puissant à la tête d'un régime fantoche, mais, en plus, Mussolini détestait l'eau et donc le lac, devait suivre un régime strict à cause de ses maux d'estomac et partager sa vie entre son épouse et sa maîtresse. Mais le temps a passé et tout cela n'a plus guère d'importance – la Villa Feltrinelli, jadis résidence d'été des membres de la dynastie du bois et de l'édition du même nom, a été transformée en un hôtel dont l'élégance luxueuse n'exclut pas l'atmosphère familiale et détendue. Babey Moulton Jue & Booth, qui ont le sens de l'Histoire, ont restauré la maison dans les règles de l'art et de l'architecture et l'ont décorée des plus belles antiquités. On trouve ici des miroirs vénitiens, de hautes cheminées et des lampes en verre soufflé (sept chambres possèdent même des fresques de plafond réalisées par les frères Lieti au cours des années 1890). La bibliothèque offre des éditions vintage du « National Geographic » et, au bar, les boissons sont servies dans des verres datant des années 1950. Le soir, on se régale d'une cuisine italienne si subtile qu'elle a même une étoile au Michelin – on le voit : Mussolini et son régime, tout cela est bien loin.

**Livre à emporter : « Crépuscule sur l'Italie » de D. H. Lawrence.**

| | |
|---|---|
| ANREISE | Am Westufer des Gardasees gelegen, 90 km vom Flughafen Verona entfernt. |
| PREISE | Zimmer ab 900 €, inklusive Frühstück (2 Nächte Mindestaufenthalt). |
| ZIMMER | 21 Zimmer und Suiten. |
| KÜCHE | Noch atmosphärischer als »The Dining Room« ist »The Pergola« im venezianischen Stil. |
| GESCHICHTE | Die Villa wurde 1892 von Alberico Barbiano di Belgioioso erbaut und 1997 vom US-Hotelier Bob Burns erworben. Das Hotel besteht seit 2001. |
| X-FAKTOR | Die musikalischen Soireen am Bösendorfer-Flügel im Salon. |

| | |
|---|---|
| ACCÈS | Sur la rive ouest du lac de Garde, à 90 km de l'aéroport de Vérone. |
| PRIX | Chambre à partir de 900 €, petit-déjeuner inclus (séjour minimum : 2 nuits). |
| CHAMBRES | 21 chambres et suites. |
| RESTAURATION | Le restaurant « The Pergola » dans le style vénetien a encore plus de charme que « The Dining Room ». |
| HISTOIRE | Construite en 1892 par Alberico Barbiano di Belgioioso, la villa a été achetée en 1997 par l'hôtelier américain Bob Burns. L'hôtel existe depuis 2001. |
| LES « PLUS » | Les soirées musicales au salon, au son du piano à queue de Bösendorfer. |

For the Fashion Conscious
Villa Amistà, near Verona

# Villa Amistà, near Verona

### For the Fashion Conscious

Fashion designers love luxury hotels – not just as glamorous accommodation during a fashion week or as stylish holiday homes, but also as design objects. Be it Christian Lacroix, who put his stamp on a Parisian boutique hotel, Rosita Missoni, who produces zigzag patterns in Edinburgh to rival the tartans, or Oscar de la Renta, who gave the Dominican Republic its most elegant resort: creators of fashion are just as successful at interior design as they are at the catwalk. The lesser brands, too, are causing a stir – among them the Italian label Byblos, whose founder Dino Facchini has opened Villa Amistà in cooperation with the architect Alessandro Mendini. It is every bit as chic, sexy and extravagant as can be expected of design "all'italiana". Behind the classical façade lie showrooms for classic furniture designs and art of the 20th century. Eero Aarnio's Ball Chair, Ron Arad's Soft Little Heavy lounge chair, the sofa named Kiss that Studio 65 designed in homage to Dalí's version of Mae West's lips. Vanessa Beecroft's photos of naked, red-headed girls, Robert Indiana's Love sculpture and dizzyingly beautiful mirrors by Anish Kapoor – every detail is design, and even the cutlery in the restaurant is by Gio Ponti. As a guest it feels like being in a museum, and often in Wonderland, but why not let go and be overwhelmed? In Villa Amistà it is easy to see why designers love luxury hotels: they are, quite simply, fun.
**Book to pack: "It's Getting Later All the Time" by Antonio Tabucchi.**

**Byblos Art Hotel Villa Amistà**
Via Cedrare 78
37020 Corrubbio di Negarine
Italy
Tel. +39 045 685 5555
Fax +39 045 685 5500
info@byblosarthotel.com
www.byblosarthotel.com
**Open all year round**

| | |
|---|---|
| DIRECTIONS | North of Verona, 11 miles from the airport. |
| RATES | Rooms from 226 €, suites from 429 €, including breakfast. |
| ROOMS | 49 rooms and 11 suites. |
| FOOD | "Atelier" with its idyllic terrace serves creative Italian cuisine. |
| HISTORY | The villa with its façade by Michele Sanmicheli dates from the 15th century. The hotel opened in September 2005. |
| X-FACTOR | The Chenot Spa, which combines Chinese and Western indulgence. |

## Für Modebewusste

Modedesigner lieben Luxushotels. Nicht nur als glamouröse Unterkünfte während einer Fashionweek oder als stilvolle Feriendomizile – sondern auch als Designobjekte. Ob Christian Lacroix, der einem Pariser Boutiquehotel seine Handschrift verlieh, Rosita Missoni, die in Edinburgh mit Zickzackmustern den Schottenkaros Konkurrenz macht, oder Oscar de la Renta, welcher der Dominikanischen Republik ihr elegantestes Resort gab: Modemacher sind als Innenarchitekten ebenso erfolgreich wie rund um den Laufsteg. Und auch kleinere Marken machen von sich reden – unter ihnen das italienische Label Byblos, dessen Gründer Dino Facchini gemeinsam mit dem Architekten Alessandro Mendini die Villa Amistà eröffnet hat. Sie ist so schick, sexy und extravagant, wie man sich Design »all'italiana« nur vorstellen kann – hinter der klassischen Fassade öffnen sich Showrooms für Möbel- und Kunstklassiker des 20. Jahrhunderts. Der Ball Chair von Eero Aarnio, der Soft Little Heavy-Loungestuhl von Ron Arad, das Kussmundsofa, das Studio 65 als Hommage an Dalís Lippen der Mae West entwarf. Vanessa Beecrofts Fotos rothaariger nackter Mädchen, Robert Indianas Love-Skulptur und Spiegel von Anish Kapoor, die schwindelerregend schön sind – jedes Detail ist Design, selbst das Restaurantbesteck stammt von Gio Ponti. Man fühlt sich manchmal wie im Museum und oft wie im Wunderland, aber warum sollte man sich hier nicht überwältigen lassen? In der Villa Amistà lässt sich nachvollziehen, warum Modedesigner Luxushotels lieben: Sie machen einfach Spaß.
**Buchtipp: »Es wird immer später« von Antonio Tabucchi.**

## Le rendez-vous des branchés

Les designers de mode adorent les hôtels de luxe. Non seulement ils y trouvent un logement glamour, le temps de la semaine de la mode, ou y passent des vacances élégantes, mais ils les considèrent comme des objets design. Qu'il s'agisse de Christian Lacroix qui a prêté sa griffe à un hôtel-boutique parisien, de Rosita Missoni dont les motifs en zig-zag font, à Edimbourg, concurrence aux écossais traditionnels ou d'Oscar de la Renta qui a donné son plus élégant lieu de séjour à la République dominicaine : les grands couturiers ont autant de succès comme architectes d'intérieur que sur les podiums. Et des marques moins connues font aussi parler d'elles ; c'est le cas, par exemple, du label italien Byblos, dont le fondateur Dino Facchini a ouvert la Villa Amistà avec l'architecte Alessandro Mendini. Elle est aussi chic, sexy et extravagante que l'on s'imagine le design « all'italiana » – les façades classiques abritent des show-rooms présentant le mobilier et les classiques de l'art du XXe siècle. Le Ball Chair d'Eero Aarnio, le fauteuil Soft Little Heavy de Ron Arad, le canapé Bocca Marilyn dessiné par le Studio 65 et qui rend hommage au sofa Mae West de Dalí, les photos de femmes rousses nues de Vanessa Beecroft, la sculpture Love de Robert Indiana et des miroirs d'Anish Kapoor, beaux à s'en pâmer – chaque détail est pur design, même les couverts du restaurant sont signés Gio Ponti. On a quelquefois l'impression de se trouver dans un musée d'art contemporain et souvent au Pays des Merveilles, mais pourquoi ne pas se laisser subjuguer, après tout ? A la Villa Amistà, on comprend pourquoi les designers de mode aiment les hôtels de luxe – ici le plaisir est au rendez-vous.
**Livre à emporter : « Il se fait tard, de plus en plus tard » d'Antonio Tabucchi.**

| | |
|---|---|
| ANREISE | Nördlich von Verona gelegen, 18 km vom Flughafen entfernt. |
| PREISE | Zimmer ab 226 €, Suite ab 429 €, inklusive Frühstück. |
| ZIMMER | 49 Zimmer und 11 Suiten. |
| KÜCHE | Im »Atelier« mit idyllischer Terrasse steht kreative italienische Küche auf der Karte. |
| GESCHICHTE | Die Villa mit ihrer Fassade von Michele Sanmicheli stammt aus dem 15. Jahrhundert. Im September 2005 eröffnete das Hotel. |
| X-FAKTOR | Das Chenot-Spa, das chinesische und westliche Wellness verbindet. |

| | |
|---|---|
| ACCÈS | Au nord de Vérone, à 18 km de l'aéroport. |
| PRIX | Chambre à partir de 226 €, suite à partir de 429 €, petit-déjeuner inclus. |
| CHAMBRES | 49 chambres et 11 suites. |
| RESTAURATION | Une gamme de plats italiens innovants à l'« Atelier » qui est doté d'une terrasse idyllique. |
| HISTOIRE | La villa avec sa façade de Michele Sanmicheli date du XVe siècle. L'hôtel est ouvert depuis septembre 2005. |
| LES « PLUS » | Le spa Chenot qui marie les traditions médicinales chinoises et occidentales. |

2004: 24 HOURS NIGHT (TELL ME, WHERE THE COLOURS HAVE GONE???)

The Love of his Life
Locanda Cipriani, Torcello

# Locanda Cipriani, Torcello

### The Love of his Life

He was in his late forties, on his fourth marriage and
burned out: when Ernest Hemingway arrived in Venice in
1948, he only wanted to take time out, drift around the city
and go duck-hunting in the lagoon. It was almost ten years
since he had written anything original. He urgently needed
inspiration for a new, major work. And he found it – in the
shape of Adriana Ivancich, in the bloom of youth (not yet
twenty), extremely pretty and so enchanting that he fell
in love with her on the spot. It was the unlikeliest and
unhappiest love of his life, but it gave him one of his great-
est successes: Hemingway paid a passionate literary tribute
to Adriana and Venice in "Across the River and into the
Trees". He wrote part of the novel in the city – in Locanda
Cipriani, where he stayed while in Venice. This guesthouse
on the little island of Torcello belonged to Giuseppe Cipriani,
the founder of "Harry's Bar", whom Hemingway had got
to know on an earlier trip to Italy. Locanda Cipriani is still
owned by the family today, and has remained down-to-earth
and likeable despite having many celebrated guests. The
rooms are plain by Venetian standards, and the cooking is
among the best in the region. When the weather is good it
is essential to book a table in the garden – amidst lush
greenery the mood is so romantic that it is easy to understand Hemingway: in Venice you have to live your love,
even though it may be unhappy.

Book to pack: "Across the River and into the Trees" by
Ernest Hemingway.

---

**Locanda Cipriani**
Piazza Santa Fosca 29
30142 Torcello – Venezia
Italy
Tel. +39 041 730 150
Fax +39 041 735 433
info@locandacipriani.com
www.locandacipriani.com
**Open all year round, except
for three weeks in January**

| | |
|---|---|
| DIRECTIONS | Torcello is in the north of the lagoon, 40 min by boat from St Mark's Square in Venice. |
| RATES | Rooms from 100 €, including breakfast. |
| ROOMS | 6 rooms. |
| FOOD | Italian cooking enhanced with garden herbs. The risotto "alla Torcellana" is legendary. |
| HISTORY | Giuseppe Cipriani opened a shop for wine and oil here in 1934 and extended it to make his Locanda in 1935. Today his grandson runs the place. |
| X-FACTOR | A walk to the church of Santa Maria Assunta with its fantastic mosaics. |

## Eine Liebe fürs Leben

Er war Ende vierzig, in vierter Ehe verheiratet und ausge-
brannt: Als Ernest Hemingway 1948 nach Venedig kam,
wollte er nichts als ausspannen, sich durch die Stadt treiben
lassen und in der Lagune auf Entenjagd gehen. Seit fast
zehn Jahren hatte er nichts Bahnbrechendes mehr zu Papier
gebracht – für ein neues, ein wichtiges Werk brauchte er
dringend Inspiration. Er fand sie auch – in Gestalt von
Adriana Ivancich, blutjung (noch keine zwanzig), bildhübsch
und so bezaubernd, dass er sich auf der Stelle in sie verliebte.
Es war die unmöglichste und unglücklichste Liebe seines
Lebens, doch sie verhalf ihm zu einem seiner größten
Erfolge: In »Über den Fluss und in die Wälder« setzte
Hemingway Adriana und Venedig ein leidenschaftliches
literarisches Denkmal. Er schrieb Teile des Romans noch
vor Ort – in der Locanda Cipriani, wo er während seines
Aufenthalts wohnte. Das Gasthaus auf der stillen Insel
Torcello gehörte Giuseppe Cipriani, dem Gründer von
»Harry's Bar«, den Hemingway bei einem früheren Auf-
enthalt in Italien kennengelernt hatte. Noch heute ist die
Locanda im Besitz der Familie und trotz zahlreicher promi-
nenter Gäste bodenständig und sehr sympathisch geblieben.
Hier wohnt man in für venezianische Verhältnisse schlich-
ten Zimmern und genießt eine der delikatesten Küchen
der Region. Bei schönem Wetter ist eine Reservierung im
Garten unverzichtbar – inmitten üppigen Grüns und im
Kerzenschein ist die Atmosphäre so romantisch, dass man
Hemingway verstehen kann: In Venedig muss man jede
Liebe leben; selbst wenn es eine unglückliche sein sollte.
**Buchtipp: »Über den Fluss und in die Wälder« von Ernest
Hemingway.**

## Amour, toujours

Lorsque Ernest Hemingway arrive à Venise en 1948, il atteint
la fin de la quarantaine, a convolé pour la quatrième fois deux
ans plus tôt et est au bout du rouleau : il n'a qu'une idée, se
détendre, se laisser vivre en ville et chasser le canard dans
la lagune. Depuis dix ans, il n'a plus rien écrit de novateur et
a grand besoin d'inspiration. Il va la trouver sous les traits
d'Adriana Ivancich : elle n'a pas vingt ans, est belle à ravir
et il va en tomber immédiatement amoureux. Cette histoire
d'amour impossible, la plus malheureuse qu'il ait vécue, lui
vaudra l'un de ses plus grands succès. Dans « Au-delà du
fleuve et sous les arbres », Hemingway élève un monument
littéraire passionné à Adriana et à Venise. Il écrit des parties
du roman sur place, à la Locanda Cipriani, où il loge pendant
son séjour. La maison d'hôtes, située sur l'île paisible de
Torcello, appartenait à Giuseppe Cipriani, le fondateur de
« Harry's Bar », dont Hemingway avait fait la connaissance
lors d'un séjour précédent en Italie. La Locanda est restée aux
mains de la famille Cipriani et la présence d'hôtes célèbres
ne lui a fait perdre ni sa rusticité ni sa chaleur humaine. On
habite ici dans des chambres sobres, comparées à celles de
Venise, et on savoure une des cuisines les plus fines de la
région. Lorsque le temps est beau, il faut absolument réserver
une table dans le jardin – au milieu de la verdure luxuriante
et aux chandelles, l'atmosphère est si romantique que l'on peut
comprendre Hemingway : il faut aimer à Venise, qu'importe si
cet amour est malheureux.
**Livre à emporter : « Au-delà du fleuve et sous les arbres »
d'Ernest Hemingway.**

| | | | | |
|---|---|---|---|---|
| ANREISE | Torcello liegt im Norden der Lagune, 40 min mit dem Boot vom Markusplatz in Venedig entfernt. | | ACCÈS | L'île de Torcello est située au nord de la lagune, à 40 min en bateau de la place Saint-Marc à Venise. |
| PREISE | Zimmer ab 100 €, inklusive Frühstück. | | PRIX | Chambre à partir 100 €, petit-déjeuner inclus. |
| ZIMMER | 6 Zimmer. | | CHAMBRES | 6 chambres. |
| KÜCHE | Die italienischen Gerichte werden mit Gartenkräutern verfeinert. Legendär ist der Risotto »alla Torcellana«. | | RESTAURATION | Cuisine vénitienne réinventée, agrémentée de fines herbes du jardin. Le risoto « alla Torcellana » est légendaire. |
| GESCHICHTE | 1934 eröffnete Giuseppe Cipriani hier einen Laden für Wein und Öl – 1935 erweiterte er ihn zur Locanda. Heute führt sein Enkel das Haus. | | HISTOIRE | En 1934, Giuseppe Cipriani a ouvert ici une boutique de vins et d'huile qu'il a transformée en auberge (locanda) en 1935. Son petit-fils dirige aujourd'hui la maison. |
| X-FAKTOR | Ein Spaziergang zur Kirche Santa Maria Assunta mit ihren fantastischen Mosaiken. | | LES « PLUS » | La promenade à l'église Santa Maria Assunta ornée de sublimes mosaïques. |

# In the Heart of Venice
## Hotel Flora, Venezia

# Hotel Flora, Venezia

**In the Heart of Venice**

"What could I tell you about Venice that you don't already know?", as the painter Paul Signac once asked. Indeed, we are not just acquainted with the fine palazzi, magnificent churches and famous museums, we even know little details too: that Venice is also called "La Serenissima", that the Grand Canal is called Canal and not Canale, that a total of over 400 bridges span the canals and that the city has sunk by almost 9 inches in the last 100 years. But does that mean that we really know Venice? Probably not. Venice is a theatre where you have to look behind the scenes; a treasure chest to which you need the key. The Venetians have this key – the Romanelli family, for example, who run the pretty Hotel Flora. For their guests a journey to the heart of Venice begins in their own four walls: in the 17th century the palazzo was a school of painting whose master is said to have known the great Titian personally. The hotel interior with its stucco, ceiling beams, mahogany beds, damask wallpaper and chandeliers also tells a story of art and culture, and right next door in Palazzo Contarini Fasan there lived a lady called Desdemona, who inspired Shakespeare to write "Othello". Those who take advice from the Romanellis before they go sightseeing will explore the lagoon on board a fishing boat, go shopping in hidden galleries or enjoy Italian cooking "alla mamma" in a trattoria. The icing on the cake is to spend some time in the sequestered courtyard of Hotel Flora – the most enchanting oasis in the city.

**Book to pack: "Death in Venice" by Thomas Mann.**

**Hotel Flora**
Calle dei Bergamaschi
San Marco 2283/A
30124 Venezia
Italy
Tel. +39 041 520 58 44
Fax +39 041 522 82 17
info@hotelflora.it
www.hotelflora.it
**Open all year round**

| | |
|---|---|
| DIRECTIONS | From Venice Airport take the Alilaguna shuttle to St Mark's Square and then walk (546 yards). |
| RATES | Rooms from 120 €, including breakfast. |
| ROOMS | 43 rooms, all with bathroom and extras such as wifi. |
| FOOD | The hotel serves only Italian breakfast, but the staff are happy to give good restaurant recommendations. |
| HISTORY | The Romanelli family have been running the hotel since 1964. |
| X-FACTOR | Unusually friendly and personal service. |

## Im Herzen Venedigs

»Was könnte ich Ihnen über Venedig erzählen, was Sie nicht schon wüssten?«, fragte der Maler Paul Signac einmal. Und wirklich: Wir wissen nicht nur von den edlen Palazzi, prachtvollen Kirchen und berühmten Museen, sondern sogar kleine Details – dass Venedig auch »La Serenissima« heißt und der Canal Grande nicht Canale Grande, dass sich über alle Kanäle mehr als vierhundert Brücken spannen und dass der Boden der Stadt in den letzten hundert Jahren fast 25 Zentimeter gesunken ist. Aber bedeutet das, dass wir Venedig auch wirklich kennen? Wahrscheinlich nicht. Venedig ist ein Theater, bei dem man hinter die Kulissen sehen muss, eine Schatztruhe, zu der man den passenden Schlüssel braucht. Ihn besitzen Einheimische wie die Familie Romanelli, die das hübsche Hotel Flora führt. Für ihre Gäste beginnt die Reise zum Herzen Venedigs in den eigenen vier Mauern – im 17. Jahrhundert war der Palazzo eine Malschule, deren Leiter den großen Tizian persönlich gekannt haben soll. Von Kunst und Kultur erzählt auch das Interieur mit Deckenbalken oder Stuck, Mahagonibetten, Damasttapeten und Lüstern; und gleich nebenan steht der Palazzo Contarini Fasan, in dem einst eine Dame namens Desdemona lebte, die Shakespeare zu seinem »Othello« inspirierte. Wer sich von den Romanellis vor dem Sightseeing beraten lässt, entdeckt die Lagune an Bord eines Fischkutters, kauft in versteckten Galerien ein oder genießt in einer Trattoria italienische Küche »alla mamma«. Gekrönt wird das Glück von Momenten im verwunschenen Hof des Flora – die zauberhafteste Oase der Stadt.

**Buchtipp: »Der Tod in Venedig« von Thomas Mann.**

## Au cœur de Venise

« Que pourrais-je vous dire de Venise que vous ne sachiez déjà ? » disait le peintre Paul Signac. Et il avait raison : non seulement nous connaissons l'existence des nobles palais, des superbes églises et des musées célèbres, mais nous savons aussi que Venise est nommée la Sérénissime et que le Grand Canal la traverse, qu'elle compte plus de 400 ponts et que le niveau du sol de la ville a baissé de près de 25 centimètres au siècle dernier. Mais cela suffit-il ? Non, sans doute. Venise est un théâtre et il faut voir ce qui se passe derrière les décors, elle est une malle aux trésors dont il faut la clé. Les gens nés ici la possèdent, par exemple la famille Romanelli qui dirige le bel hôtel Flora. Pour ceux qui y séjournent, le voyage au cœur de la cité des doges commence ici – au XVII<sup>e</sup> siècle, le palais abritait une école de dessin dont le directeur aurait personnellement connu le grand Titien. Les poutres et les stucs, les lits d'acajou, les tentures de damas et les lustres étincelants nous parlent aussi d'art et de culture. Et juste à côté se dresse le palais Contarini Fasan, dit « Maison de Desdémone », celle-là même qui inspira à Shakespeare l'histoire d' « Othello ». Bien inspiré est celui qui écoute les conseils des Romanelli avant de visiter la ville : il découvre la lagune à bord d'un chalutier, fait ses achats dans des galeries bien cachées et déguste dans une trattoria la cuisine vénitienne « alla mamma ». Les instants passés dans la végétation luxuriante de la cour, l'oasis enchanteresse de la ville, ne pourront qu'ajouter à son bonheur.

**Livre à emporter : « Mort à Venise » de Thomas Mann.**

| | |
|---|---|
| ANREISE | Vom Flughafen Venedig nimmt man den Alilaguna-Shuttle zum Markusplatz und geht von dort zu Fuß (500 m). |
| PREISE | Zimmer ab 120 €, inklusive Frühstück. |
| ZIMMER | 43 Zimmer, alle mit Bad sowie Extras wie WiFi. |
| KÜCHE | Im Hotel wird nur italienisches Frühstück serviert – die Mitarbeiter geben gerne und gute Restauranttipps. |
| GESCHICHTE | Die Familie Romanelli führt das Hotel seit 1964. |
| X-FAKTOR | Der außergewöhnlich freundliche und persönliche Service. |

| | |
|---|---|
| ACCÈS | De l'aéroport de Venise, on prend la navette Alilaguna jusqu'à la place Saint-Marc. L'hôtel est à 500 m. |
| PRIX | Chambre à partir de 120 €, petit-déjeuner inclus. |
| CHAMBRES | 43 chambres avec salle de bains ainsi que des extras comme le Wi-Fi. |
| RESTAURATION | L'hôtel ne propose qu'un petit-déjeuner italien – le personnel prodigue volontiers de bonnes adresses gastronomiques. |
| HISTOIRE | La famille Romanelli dirige l'hôtel depuis 1964. |
| LES « PLUS » | Le service extrêmement aimable et personnalisé. |

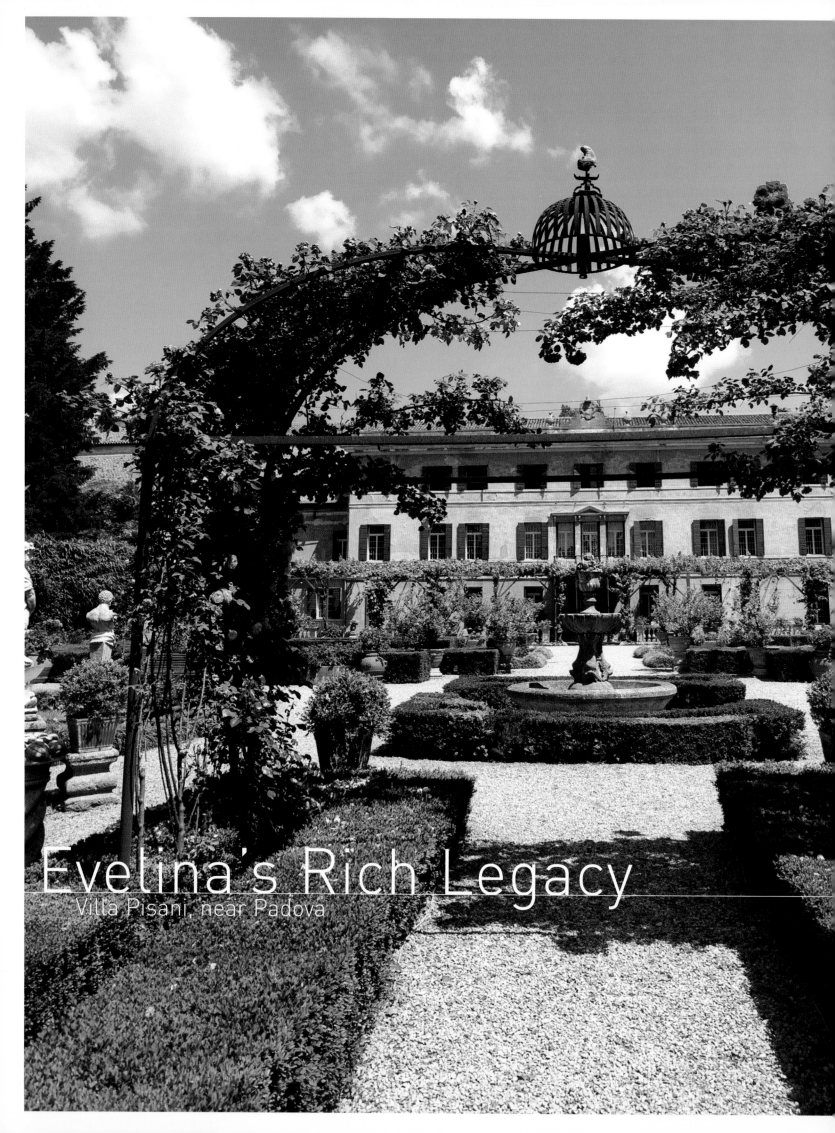

# Evelina's Rich Legacy
Villa Pisani, near Padova

# Villa Pisani, near Padova

**Evelina's Rich Legacy**

Her father was an English doctor whose patients included Lord Byron; her mother was French and had grown up in the harem of the Turkish sultan. Evelina van Millingen herself was brought up in Istanbul and Rome, with a multicultural and exotic background that she proudly displayed – her first appearance at "La Fenice" in Venice in an oriental robe was the talk of the town and opened the doors of the Italian aristocracy to her. In these circles she met Almoro Pisani III, the heir of one of the richest and noblest Venetian clans. In 1852 they married and moved into Villa Pisani, one of the most magnificent villas inspired by Palladio in the Veneto. Today guests can reside in the very same surroundings in which Evelina once received such notables as Queen Victoria. When the estate was renovated and converted into a high-class guesthouse, the original frescoes by such superb painters as Paolo Veronese and Giovanni Battista Zelotti were preserved. The rooms are furnished with antiques and have an unimpeded view of the lovely park, which Evelina laid out herself, thus combining Victorian and Italian garden design in keeping with her way of life. She so loved this green paradise that her spirit has remained there: every September, so it is said, the former lady of the house walks through the park. She cannot necessarily be seen, but can always be heard: the silk of her dress rustles softly like the leaves on the trees.

**Books to pack: "The Fugitive" by Massimo Carlotto and "Days Spent on a Doge's Farm" by Margaret Symonds (the author dedicated this work to Villa Pisani).**

**Villa Pisani, Bolognesi Scalabrin**
Via Roma 19
35040 Vescovana
Italy
Tel. +39 0425 920 016 and +39 0425 450 811
Fax +39 0425 920 016
info@villapisani.it
www.villapisani.it
**Open all year round**

| | |
|---|---|
| DIRECTIONS | South of Padua, about 52 miles from Venice Airport. |
| RATES | Rooms from 170 €, suites from 230 €, including breakfast. |
| ROOMS | 7 rooms and 1 suite (for up to 4 persons). |
| FOOD | Only breakfast is served; on warm days don't fail to enjoy it in the park! |
| HISTORY | The Pisani built the villa in the first half of the 16th century. The present owners purchased it in the late 1960s. |
| X-FACTOR | Villa and park can be reserved exclusively – for weddings, for example. |

## Evelinas reiches Erbe

Ihr Vater war ein englischer Arzt, zu dessen Patienten Lord
Byron gehörte, ihre Mutter eine Französin, die im Harem
des türkischen Sultans aufgewachsen war, und sie selbst
wurde in Istanbul sowie Rom erzogen: Evelina van Millingen
besaß so multikulturelle wie exotische Wurzeln, die sie selbst-
bewusst zur Schau stellte – ihr erster Besuch in Venedigs
»La Fenice« in einer orientalischen Robe sorgte in der ganzen
Stadt für Gesprächsstoff und öffnete ihr die Türen zum
italienischen Adel. In diesen Kreisen lernte sie Almoro III.
Pisani kennen, den Erben einer der nobelsten und reichsten
venezianischen Clans. Sie heiratete ihn 1852 und zog mit
ihm in die Villa Pisani – eine der prachtvollsten von Palladio
inspirierten Villen des Veneto. Im selben Ambiente, in dem
Evelina einst Berühmtheiten wie Queen Victoria empfing,
kann man noch heute residieren. Bei der Renovierung des
Anwesens in ein herrschaftliches Gästehaus wurden die
Originalfresken von großartigen Malern wie Paolo Veronese
und Giovanni Battista Zelotti erhalten, die Räume sind mit
Antiquitäten eingerichtet und blicken direkt in den verwunschenen Park. Ihn hatte Evelina persönlich angelegt und
dabei ihrem Lebensstil entsprechend viktorianische und
italienische Gartenkunst verbunden. Sie liebte dieses grüne
Wunderland so sehr, dass ihr Geist dort noch immer präsent
ist: Jedes Jahr im September, so erzählt man sich, wandelt
die einstige Hausherrin durch den Park. Dabei ist sie nicht
immer zu sehen, aber immer zu hören: Die Seide ihres
Kleides raschelt so sanft wie die Blätter der Bäume.
**Buchtipps: »Wo die Zitronen blühen« von Massimo Carlotto
und »Days spent on a Doge's Farm« von Margaret Symonds
(die Autorin widmete dieses Werk der Villa Pisani).**

## L'héritage d'Evelina

Son père était un médecin anglais dont lord Byron avait été
le patient, sa mère une Française qui avait grandi dans le
harem du sultan turc – elle-même fut élevée à Istanbul et
à Rome : Evelina van Millingen possédait des racines multi-
culturelles et exotiques qu'elle savait mettre en valeur – sa
première apparition en robe orientale à « La Fenice » de Venise
défraya la chronique et lui ouvrit les portes de la noblesse
italienne. Elle fit alors la connaissance d'Almoro III Pisani,
héritier d'une des familles les plus nobles et les plus fortunées
de Venise. Elle l'épousa en 1852 et s'installa avec lui dans la
Villa Pisani, une des plus splendides villas palladiennes de
Vénétie. On peut résider aujourd'hui encore dans ce cadre
où ont été reçues des célébrités comme la reine Victoria.
Lorsque la propriété a été transformée en hôtel seigneurial,
les fresques originales de peintres comme Paul Véronèse
et Giovanni Battista Zelotti ont été conservées ; les pièces
abritent des antiquités et s'ouvrent directement sur la verdure
du parc. Evelina avait conçu personnellement celui-ci, mariant
selon son mode de vie l'art des jardins victorien et italien.
Elle aimait tant ce séjour enchanteur que son esprit y est
encore présent : on raconte que l'ancienne maîtresse des
lieux se promène dans le parc chaque année en septembre.
On ne la voit pas toujours, mais on entend la soie de sa robe
bruisser aussi doucement que les feuilles des arbres.
**Livres à emporter : « Padana City » de Massimo Carlotto et
Marco Videtta et « Days spent on a Doge's Farm » de Margaret
Symonds (dédié à la Villa Pisani).**

| | |
|---|---|
| ANREISE | Südlich von Padua gelegen, rund 85 km vom Flughafen Venedig entfernt. |
| PREISE | Zimmer ab 170 €, Suite ab 230 €, inklusive Frühstück. |
| ZIMMER | 7 Zimmer und 1 Suite (diese für bis zu 4 Personen). |
| KÜCHE | Serviert wird nur Frühstück; an warmen Tagen sollte man es unbedingt im Park genießen! |
| GESCHICHTE | Die Pisanis ließen die Villa in der ersten Hälfte des 16. Jahrhunderts errichten. Die heutigen Besitzer erwarben sie in den späten 1960ern. |
| X-FAKTOR | Villa und Park können exklusiv gebucht werden, z.B. für Hochzeiten. |

| | |
|---|---|
| ACCÈS | Au sud de Padoue, à environ 85 km de l'aéroport de Venise. |
| PRIX | Chambre à partir de 170 €, suite à partir de 230 €, petit-déjeuner inclus. |
| CHAMBRES | 7 chambres et 1 suite (jusqu'à 4 personnes). |
| RESTAURATION | Petit-déjeuner uniquement ; lorsqu'il fait chaud il faut absolument le prendre dans le parc ! |
| HISTOIRE | Les Pisani ont fait édifier la villa dans la première moitié du XVIe siècle. Les propriétaires actuels l'ont achetée à la fin des années 1960. |
| LES « PLUS » | La villa et le parc peuvent être réservés en exclusivité, pour fêter un mariage par exemple. |

# At Home with the Cardinal
Al Cardinal Mazzarino, Cherasco

# Al Cardinal Mazzarino, Cherasco

**At Home with the Cardinal**

He was a child prodigy who attended the Jesuit college in Rome at the age of just five and there learned all the sermons by heart in the twinkling of an eye. In the course of his life he collected 5000 books, which laid the foundation for the first public library in Paris. And he had a passion for diamonds – the legendary Mazarin cut is named after this man: the Italian Giulio Raimondo Mazzarino (1602–1661), who went to France as the successor of Richelieu and as Cardinal Mazarin held the reins of the Sun King's realm. He was particularly successful in foreign affairs, and was considered the driving force behind the Treaty of Cherasco, which ended the War of the Mantuan Succession in 1631. He is revered in Cherasco to this day – and the most stylish place to honour him is the Hotel Al Cardinal Mazzarino, a historic building that three women friends have styled like a country house in the middle of the town. Inside, antiques and meadow flowers create a rustic atmosphere (guests who occupy the Suite del Cardinale even have an open fireplace), and the secluded garden is an oasis where roses, lilacs, camellias and even palms thrive. On warm days no one should fail to have breakfast and dinner in these green surroundings – Amelia, the cook, works her magic with old recipes from the Langhe region, and the sommelière Mariangela serves wines to complement the food. When the weather is cooler, the restaurant is moved into the library, where of course there is literature to suit the hotel: entertaining books about the life of Cardinal Mazarin.

**Books to pack: "The Island of the Day Before" by Umberto Eco and "Twenty Years After" by Alexandre Dumas (Cardinal Mazarin plays a leading role in both books).**

---

**Al Cardinal Mazzarino**
Via San Pietro 48
12062 Cherasco
Italy
Tel. +39 0172 488 364
Mobile +39 338 828 4913
info@cardinalmazzarino.com
www.cardinalmazzarino.com
**Open all year round, except between
January 7 and February 13**

| | |
|---|---|
| DIRECTIONS | In the centre of Cherasco, 34 miles from Turin, 130 miles from Milan. |
| RATES | Rooms from 150 €, including breakfast. |
| ROOMS | 2 rooms and 1 suite. |
| FOOD | The restaurant serves regional cooking, always fresh, and is also open to non-residents. |
| HISTORY | The building dates from the Middle Ages and was later used as a Carmelite monastery. The hotel has existed in its current form since 2006 and is managed by Marinella Aiassa. |
| X-FACTOR | The breakfast for late risers with cake warm from the oven and home-made jam. |

## Zu Gast beim Kardinal

Er war ein Wunderkind, das schon mit fünf Jahren das Jesuitenkolleg in Rom besuchte und dort alle Predigten im Handumdrehen auswendig lernte. Er trug im Lauf seines Lebens 5.000 Bücher zusammen, die zum Grundstock der ältesten öffentlichen Bibliothek von Paris wurden. Und er besaß eine Leidenschaft für Diamanten – der legendäre Mazarinschliff verdankt ihm seinen Namen: Der Italiener Giulio Raimondo Mazzarino (1602–1661), der als Nachfolger Richelieus nach Frankreich ging und dort als Kardinal Mazarin das Reich des Sonnenkönigs lenkte. In der Außenpolitik war er dabei besonders erfolgreich – so galt er als treibende Kraft hinter dem Frieden von Cherasco, der 1631 den Mantuanischen Erbfolgekrieg beendete. In Cherasco verehrt man Mazarin deshalb noch heute – am schönsten im Hotel Al Cardinal Mazzarino. Drei Freundinnen haben das historische Gebäude wie ein privates Landhaus mitten in der Stadt gestaltet: Innen sorgen Antiquitäten sowie Wiesenblumen für rustikales Flair (Gäste der »Suite del Cardinale« besitzen sogar einen offenen Kamin), und der verwunschene Garten ist eine Oase, in der Rosen, Flieder, Kamelien, selbst Palmen gedeihen. An warmen Tagen sollte man Frühstück und Abendessen unbedingt im Grünen genießen – Köchin Amelia zaubert nach alten Rezepten Spezialitäten der Langhe, und Sommelière Mariangela serviert die passenden Weine dazu. Herrschen kältere Temperaturen, wird das Restaurant in die Bibliothek verlegt, in der natürlich die zum Haus passende Literatur zu finden ist: Spannende Titel über das Leben des Kardinals Mazarin.
**Buchtipps: »Die Insel des vorigen Tages« von Umberto Eco und »Zwanzig Jahre später« von Alexandre Dumas (in beiden Büchern spielt Kardinal Mazarin eine Hauptrolle).**

## Son Éminence invite

Génie en herbe, l'Italien Giulio Raimondo Mazzarino (1602–1661) fréquentait, dès l'âge de cinq ans, le collège romain des jésuites et apprit par cœur tous les sermons en un tour de main. Grand collectionneur de livres – les 5000 volumes qu'il a rassemblés sont la base de la plus ancienne bibliothèque publique de Paris – il avait aussi la passion des diamants et la célèbre « taille Mazarin » lui doit son nom. Après avoir été au service du pape, il éveilla l'intérêt de Richelieu qui le retint auprès de lui et le recommanda à Louis XIII, qui le nomma ministre. Le point fort du cardinal Mazarin, ainsi qu'il se nomme ensuite, était la politique extérieure – n'était-il pas le principal initiateur du traité de Cherasco qui mit fin, en 1631, à la guerre de Succession de Mantoue ? En tout cas, on le vénère aujourd'hui encore à Cherasco, et de manière particulièrement esthétique à l'Hotel Al Cardinal Mazzarino, un bâtiment historique que trois amies ont aménagé comme une maison de campagne : à l'intérieur, des antiquités et des fleurs des champs génèrent une ambiance rustique (la « Suite del Cardinal » possède même une cheminée) et le jardin est un lieu enchanté où fleurissent les roses, le lilas, les camélias – on y trouve même des palmiers. Lorsqu'il fait chaud, il faut absolument prendre son petit-déjeuner et son dîner dans la verdure – la cuisinière Amelia, détentrice de vieilles recettes, concocte des spécialités des Langhe et la sommelière Mariangela sert les vins correspondant aux plats. Si les températures baissent, on se restaure dans la bibliothèque qui abrite bien sûr les livres adaptés à l'esprit des lieux, des ouvrages retraçant la vie du cardinal Mazarin.
**Livres à emporter : « L'Ile du jour d'avant » d'Umberto Eco et « Vingt ans après » d'Alexandre Dumas (le cardinal Mazarin y joue un rôlr majeur).**

| | |
|---|---|
| ANREISE | Im Zentrum von Cherasco gelegen, 55 km von Turin, 210 km von Mailand entfernt. |
| PREISE | Zimmer ab 150 €, inklusive Frühstück. |
| ZIMMER | 2 Zimmer und 1 Suite. |
| KÜCHE | Das Restaurant mit immer frischen regionalen Menüs steht auch externen Gästen offen. |
| GESCHICHTE | Erbaut wurde das Haus im Mittelalter, später diente es als Karmeliterkloster. Das Hotel in seiner heutigen Form besteht seit 2006 und wird von Marinella Aiassa geleitet. |
| X-FAKTOR | Das Langschläferfrühstück mit ofenwarmem Kuchen und hausgemachter Marmelade. |

| | |
|---|---|
| ACCÈS | Au centre de Cherasco, à 55 km de Turin et 210 km de Milan. |
| PRIX | Chambre à partir de 150 €, petit-déjeuner inclus. |
| CHAMBRES | 2 chambres et 1 suite. |
| RESTAURATION | La cuisine régionale proposée régalera aussi ceux qui ne séjournent pas à l'hôtel. |
| HISTOIRE | Construite au Moyen Âge, la maison a abrité plus tard un couvent de carmélites. Sous sa forme actuelle, l'hôtel existe depuis 2006 et est dirigé par Marinella Aiassa. |
| LES « PLUS » | Le petit-déjeuner proposé aux lève-tard – gâteaux sortant du four et confitures maison. |

# Homage to a Landscape
Antico Borgo del Riondino, near Cuneo

# Antico Borgo del Riondino, near Cuneo

### Homage to a Landscape

Some settlements seem always to have existed. They fit into the countryside as a matter of course, so that the boundaries between nature and architecture are blurred. They possess such timeless beauty that past and present seem to merge. Antico Borgo del Riondino is just such a place – a grouping of medieval houses on a hill in the Langhe region, which the architect Marco Poncellini has converted into his studio and an agritourism. In doing so he used traditional methods wherever possible, preserving historic masonry and ceiling joists but at the same time combining the old structure with modern elements. Façades of tall windows let in plenty of light, black ceramic tiles accentuate ancient stone or wooden floors, crystal chandeliers are suspended above heavy beds and design washbasins collect the water from old-fashioned taps. The interior is both simple and sophisticated, highly sensuous and sometimes almost poetic – and it matches the exterior perfectly. The ten-hectare park, a wonderland of meadows, woods and vineyards, extends across the hills of three valleys. Aromatic nuts, figs and rosemary thrive here – specialities of the Langhe that are used in the agritourism's own kitchen. Marco Poncellini's father gave up his career as a banker to be the chef here and cook to regional recipes. So even the food fits in with the overall concept and makes the Riondino an all-round work of art – and an act of homage to the landscape.

**Book to pack: "A Private Affair" by Beppe Fenoglio.**

**Antico Borgo del Riondino**
Via dei Fiori 13
12050 Trezzo Tinella
Italy
Tel. +39 0173 630 313
Fax +39 0173 630 329
borgodelriondino@libero.it
www.riondino.it
**Open from Easter to December**

| | |
|---|---|
| DIRECTIONS | In the south of Piedmont, 71 miles from Turin Airport. |
| RATES | Rooms from 120 €, including breakfast. |
| ROOMS | 8 rooms. |
| FOOD | Picnics in the park can be recommended as highly as dinner. |
| HISTORY | The first map that shows the estate dates from the year AD 1000. The medieval farm buildings were used in the First and Second World Wars as a prisoner-of-war camp and partisan base; the Poncellinis opened the agritourism in 1988. |
| X-FACTOR | The simple chapel in the park. |

## Hommage an eine Landschaft

Es gibt Siedlungen, die schon immer da gewesen zu sein scheinen. Die sich so selbstverständlich in eine Landschaft einfügen, dass die Grenzen zwischen Natur und Architektur verwischen, und die so zeitlos schön sind, dass auch Geschichte und Gegenwart ineinander übergehen. Solch ein Ort ist der Antico Borgo del Riondino – eine Sammlung mittelalterlicher Häuser auf einem Hügel der Langhe, die der Architekt Marco Poncellini zu seinem Atelier und zu einem Agriturismo umgebaut hat. Wo immer möglich, arbeitete er dabei nach traditionellen Techniken und erhielt historische Mauern sowie Deckenbalken – gleichzeitig kombinierte er die alte Struktur aber mit modernen Elementen. So lassen hohe Fensterfronten viel Licht in die Räume, schwarze Keramikkacheln akzentuieren antike Stein- oder Holzböden, über schweren Betten schweben Kristalllüster, und unter altmodischen Wasserhähnen stehen Designerbecken. Das Interieur ist schlicht und sophisticated zugleich, sehr sinnlich und manchmal fast poetisch – und passt damit perfekt zum Exterieur: Der zehn Hektar große Park verläuft über die Hügel dreier Täler und ist ein Wunderland aus Wiesen, Wäldern und Weinbergen. Hier gedeihen aromatische Nüsse, Feigen und Rosmarin – Spezialitäten der Langhe, die im hauseigenen Restaurant Verwendung finden. Marco Poncellinis Vater gab seine Karriere als Banker auf, um hier am Herd zu stehen und nach regionalen Rezepten zu kochen. Selbst die Küche fügt sich also ins Konzept und macht den Riondino zu einem Gesamtkunstwerk – und zu einer Hommage an eine Landschaft.
**Buchtipp: »Eine Privatsache« von Beppe Fenoglio.**

## Hommage à un paysage

Certaines agglomérations rurales semblent avoir toujours existé. Elles sont si naturellement intégrées au paysage que les limites entre la nature et l'architecture s'estompent, et d'une beauté si intemporelle que le passé et le présent se marient sous nos yeux. L'Antico Borgo del Riondino – un bourg médiéval implanté sur une colline des Langhe, que Marco Poncellini a transformé en atelier et centre agrotouristique – est l'un de ces endroits. Les techniques traditionnelles ont été utilisées partout où cela était possible, les murs historiques et les poutres des plafonds on été conservés, mais en combinant la structure ancienne à des éléments modernes. De vastes baies vitrées laissent la lumière pénétrer dans les pièces, des carreaux de céramique noirs accentuent l'effet des sols anciens en pierre ou en bois, des lustres de cristal sont suspendus au-dessus de lits massifs et des robinets vieillots surplombent des lavabos design. L'intérieur est à la fois sobre et sophistiqué, très sensuel et parfois presque poétique, en parfaite harmonie avec le paysage qui l'entoure : le parc de dix hectares qui s'étend sur les collines de trois vallées est une merveille de prairies, de forêts et de vignes. On y récolte des noix, des figues et du romarin, spécialités des Langhe que propose le restaurant de la maison. Le père de Marco Poncellini a abandonné une carrière de banquier pour passer derrière les fourneaux et cuisiner des recettes de la région. Ainsi, même la cuisine est partie du concept et fait du Riondino une œuvre d'art totale et un hommage au paysage.
**Livre à emporter : « Une Affaire personnelle » de Beppe Fenoglio.**

| | | | |
|---|---|---|---|
| ANREISE | Im Süden des Piemont gelegen, 115 km vom Flughafen Turin entfernt. | ACCÈS | Au sud du Piémont, à 115 km de l'aéroport de Turin. |
| PREISE | Zimmer ab 120 €, inklusive Frühstück. | PRIX | Chambre à partir de 120 €, petit-déjeuner inclus. |
| ZIMMER | 8 Zimmer. | CHAMBRES | 8 chambres. |
| KÜCHE | Ebenso empfehlenswert wie die Dinner sind die Picknicks im Park. | RESTAURATION | Les pique-niques dans le parc sont aussi délicieux que les dîners. |
| GESCHICHTE | Die älteste Karte, auf der das Grundstück eingezeichnet ist, stammt aus dem Jahr 1000 n. Chr. Die mittelalterlichen Höfe dienten im Ersten und Zweiten Weltkrieg als Gefangenenlager und Partisanenbasis. 1988 eröffneten die Poncellinis das Agriturismo. | HISTOIRE | La première carte indiquant le site date de l'an 1000 de notre ère. Les fermes médiévales ont servi de camps de prisonniers et de base aux partisans pendant la Première et la Seconde Guerre mondiale ; les Poncellini ont ouvert le site agrotouristique en 1988. |
| X-FAKTOR | Die schlichte Parkkapelle unter freiem Himmel. | LES « PLUS » | La sobre chapelle du parc. |

# Land of Plenty
Relais San Maurizio, near Cuneo

# Relais San Maurizio, near Cuneo

**Land of Plenty**

You only have to say the name, and the eyes of bon viveurs and gourmets light up: the Langhe is the culinary heart of northern Italy, a luxurious land of plenty. On its hills grow the Nebbiolo grapes, whose name tells of autumn mist ("nebbia") in the valleys; these are the grapes from which the ruby-red Barolo and Barbaresco wines are pressed. In the woods of the Langhe the "tuber magnatum pico" lies hidden: the white Alba truffle that Cicero enthused about long ago and European crowned heads have prized for centuries. Thanks to their seductive aroma, these tubers in mottled colours of cream and nut transform even the simplest dish into a delicacy. They are considered the best and most expensive truffles in the world – in 2007 a fanatical gourmet bought a 750-gram truffle for 143,000 euros at auction in Alba. But this "white gold" can also be acquired for more moderate prices, for example in the restaurant of Relais San Maurizio, a former Franciscan monastery that is today home to a wonderful Relais & Châteaux hotel. Here culinary treats are served in a vaulted cellar that is every bit as atmospheric as the rooms, which were created from former monks' cells. For all its creature comforts, the estate has preserved its contemplative peace: guests can walk beneath ancient trees in the park, enjoy relaxing salt treatments in the spa designed by Sandro Sergi and gaze across the vineyards from the pool. A stay in the Langhe could not offer more enjoyment.

**Book to pack: "This Business of Living" by Cesare Pavese.**

| **Relais San Maurizio** | | |
|---|---|---|
| Località San Maurizio 39 | DIRECTIONS | 71 miles from Turin Airport. |
| 12058 Santo Stefano Belbo | RATES | Rooms from 280 €, suites from 400 €, breakfast 20 €. |
| Italy | ROOMS | 31 rooms and suites. |
| Tel. +39 0141 841 900 | FOOD | "Da Guido" restaurant has a Michelin star, the "Hemingway" bar pays homage to the writer, who loved Italy. |
| Fax +39 0141 843 833 | | |
| info@relaissanmaurizio.it | | |
| www.relaissanmaurizio.it | HISTORY | The monastery was built in 1619, and from 1862 the counts of Santo Stefano Belbo lived here. The hotel opened in 2002. |
| **Open from the beginning of March to the end of December** | X-FACTOR | True fans can go truffle-hunting with a "trifolau" (truffle expert). |

## Im Schlaraffenland

Man muss nur einmal ihren Namen aussprechen – und
schon bekommen Genießer und Gourmets glänzende
Augen: Die Langhe sind das kulinarische Herz Norditaliens,
ein Schlaraffenland de luxe. Auf ihren Hügeln wachsen die
Nebbiolo-Trauben, die vom herbstlichen Nebel (»nebbia«)
in den Tälern erzählen und aus denen die rubinroten Weine
Barolo und Barbaresco gekeltert werden. Und in ihren
Wäldern versteckt sich der »Tuber Magnatum Pico« – der
weiße Alba-Trüffel, von dem schon Cicero schwärmte und
den Friedrich I. von Preußen höchstpersönlich suchte. Die
creme- und nussfarben marmorierten Knollen verwandeln
dank ihres verführerischen Aromas selbst die schlichtesten
Speisen in Delikatessen; sie gelten als die besten und
teuersten Trüffeln der Welt – im Jahr 2007 ersteigerte ein
fanatischer Feinschmecker in Alba einen 750-Gramm-Trüffel
für 143.000 Euro. Doch das »weiße Gold« lässt sich auch
zu gemäßigteren Preisen genießen: zum Beispiel im
Restaurant des Relais San Maurizio, einem ehemaligen
Franziskanerkloster, das heute ein wunderschönes Relais-&-
Châteaux-Hotel beherbergt. Hier werden die Köstlichkeiten
im Gewölbekeller serviert – er ist ebenso stimmungsvoll wie
die Zimmer, die aus den einstigen Mönchszellen entstanden
sind. Bei allem Komfort hat sich das Anwesen eine kontem-
plative Ruhe bewahrt: Im Park wandelt man unter uralten
Bäumen, im Spa des Designers Sandro Sergi entspannen
Salzanwendungen, und vom Pool aus schweift der Blick
über die Weinberge – genussvoller kann ein Aufenthalt in
den Langhe nicht sein.

**Buchtipp: »Das Handwerk des Lebens« von Cesare Pavese.**

## Le pays de cocagne

Rien que leur nom fait briller les yeux des gourmets et
des bons vivants : les Langhe sont le cœur gastronomique
de l'Italie du Nord, une région où règne l'abondance. Sur
ses collines pousse le nebbiolo, un cépage dont le nom
(« nebbia ») évoque la brume automnale et qui composera
le barolo et le barbaresco couleur de rubis. Et dans les forêts
se cache la « tuber magnatum pico », la truffe blanche du
Piémont, dont Cicéron chantait déjà les louanges et que
Frédéric Iᵉʳ de Prusse allait chercher en personne. L'arôme
subtil de l'« enfant de la terre » aux marbrures crème et
noisette  transforme les plats les plus sobres en mets exquis ;
elle est la meilleure truffe du monde et la plus chère – en
2007, un amateur d'Alba n'a pas hésité à débourser 143 000
euros pour une truffe de 750 grammes. Mais il est possible
d'y goûter à des prix plus abordables, par exemple au restaurant du Relais San Maurizio, un ancien monastère franciscain
qui abrite aujourd'hui un magnifique hôtel faisant partie
des Relais & Châteaux. On peut la déguster sous les voûtes,
dans un cadre aussi impressionnant que celui des chambres
qui étaient autrefois les cellules des moines. En dépit des
changements apportés pour assurer le confort des clients,
le domaine a su conserver son atmosphère paisible, propice
à la méditation : on peut se promener dans le parc aux
arbres ancestraux et profiter de soins au sel dans le spa
conçu par le designer Sandro Sergi. De la piscine, le regard
effleure les vignobles – un séjour dans les Langhe ne saurait
être plus agréable.

**Livre à emporter : « Le Métier de vivre » de Cesare Pavese.**

| | |
|---|---|
| ANREISE | 115 km vom Flughafen Turin entfernt. |
| PREISE | Zimmer ab 280 €, Suite ab 400 €, Frühstück 20 €. |
| ZIMMER | 31 Zimmer und Suiten. |
| KÜCHE | Das Restaurant »Da Guido« hat einen Michelin-Stern, die »Hemingway«-Bar ist eine Hommage an den Schrift-steller, der Italien liebte. |
| GESCHICHTE | Das Kloster wurde 1619 erbaut, ab 1862 lebten hier die Grafen von Santo Stefano Belbo. Das Hotel eröffnete 2002. |
| X-FAKTOR | Echte Fans können einen »trifolau« (Trüffelexperte) bei der Suche begleiten. |

| | |
|---|---|
| ACCÈS | Situé à 115 km de l'aéroport de Turin. |
| PRIX | Chambre à partir de 280 €, suite à partir de 400 €, petit-déjeuner 20 €. |
| CHAMBRES | 31 chambres et suites. |
| RESTAURATION | Le restaurant « Da Guido » a une étoile au Michelin, le bar « Hemingway » rend hommage à l'écrivain, amoureux de l'Italie. |
| HISTOIRE | Construit en 1619, le monastère est devenu à partir de 1862 la résidence des comtes de Santo Stefano Belbo. L'hôtel a ouvert ses portes en 2002. |
| LES « PLUS » | Les amateurs de truffes peuvent accompagner un « trifolau » qui connaît les bons endroits. |

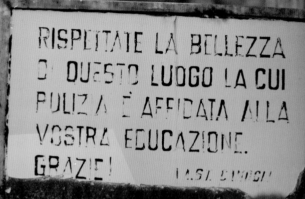

In the Wake of Seafarers

Stella Maris, Punta Chiappa

# Stella Maris, Punta Chiappa

**In the Wake of Seafarers**

A picturesque harbour, colourful houses and a superb sea view – at first sight Camogli seems like just one more pretty village on the Ligurian coast. The place may be small, but it has history on a grand scale: in the Middle Ages its powerful fleet gave it the title "town of a thousand white sails" and even in the late 19th century, 500 of its 12,000 residents were registered sea captains. Its nautical history is kept alive today by festivals such as the "Sagra del Pesce" in May, when fish is fried for everyone in gigantic pans in the piazza, and by the "Stella Maris" procession of ships in honour of the Virgin Mary, patron of all seafarers: on the first Sunday in August hundreds of boats set course for Punta Chiappa, a nearby promontory on which an altar to the Virgin stands. To see the action right up close when the boats anchor, the Stella Maris is the place – the hotel, built high on the cliffs incorporating an old monastery, commands a breathtaking view. Don't fail to book in time, however, as the house has just 12 rooms, which are furnished in a pleasant but charming style with tiled floors, four-poster beds and antiques. The restaurant, too, where the regional dishes are simple but delicious, concentrates on essentials. The food is served on a terrace with a sea view – especially beautiful on the evening of the procession, when countless floating candles are placed on the water at dusk to transform the Golfo Paradiso into a sea of lights.

**Book to pack: "Childe Harold's Pilgrimage" by Lord Byron.**

| | |
|---|---|
| **Stella Maris** | |
| Via San Nicolò 68 | |
| Punta Chiappa | |
| 16032 Camogli | |
| Italy | |
| Tel. +39 0185 770 285 | |
| Fax +39 0331 264 864 | |
| stellamaris@cssitalia.it | |
| www.stellamaris.cc | |
| **Open all year round** | |

| | |
|---|---|
| DIRECTIONS | Camogli lies 18 miles from Genoa; from the harbour the boat transfer takes 10 minutes, the climb up stone steps to the hotel about 7 min. Not accessible by car! |
| RATES | Rooms from 75 €, suites from 115 €, including breakfast. |
| ROOMS | 12 rooms. |
| FOOD | Down-to-earth Ligurian meals – freshly prepared. |
| HISTORY | Lord Byron made the hotel famous when he lived and wrote here in 1821. It was comprehensively refurbished in early 2009. |
| X-FACTOR | The sequestered garden. |

## Den Seefahrern auf der Spur

Ein pittoresker Hafen, bunte Häuser und eine herrliche Sicht übers Meer – auf den ersten Blick wirkt Camogli nur wie ein weiteres hübsches Dorf an der Küste Liguriens. Doch der kleine Ort hat eine große Geschichte: Im Mittelalter war er dank seiner mächtigen Flotte als »Stadt der tausend weißen Segel« bekannt, und noch Ende des 19. Jahrhunderts waren 500 seiner 12.000 Einwohner als Kapitäne registriert. An die nautisch geprägte Historie erinnern heute Feste wie die »Sagra del Pesce« im Mai, bei der in riesigen Pfannen auf der Piazza Fisch für alle gebraten wird, und die Boots-prozession »Stella Maris« zu Ehren Marias, der Schutzpatronin aller Seefahrer: Am ersten Augustsonntag nehmen Hunderte von Schiffen Kurs auf Punta Chiappa – eine nahe Land-zunge, auf der ein Marienaltar steht. Wer das Ankern der Boote aus nächster Nähe erleben möchte, kann dies vom Stella Maris aus tun – das Hotel entstand aus einem alten Kloster und hat hoch über den Klippen gelegen eine atembe-raubende Sicht. Beim Buchen muss man allerdings schnell sein, denn das Haus besitzt nur zwölf Zimmer, die mit Fliesenböden, Himmelbetten und Antiquitäten schlicht, aber sehr charmant eingerichtet sind. Aufs Wesentliche konzen-triert sich auch das Restaurant, dessen regionale Menüs so einfach wie köstlich sind. Serviert werden sie auf der Terrasse mit Meerblick – und dieser ist am Abend der Prozession besonders schön: Mit Einbruch der Dunkelheit werden ungezählte Schwimmkerzen aufs Wasser gesetzt und ver-wandeln den Golfo Paradiso in ein Lichtermeer.

**Buchtipp: »Childe Harolds Pilgerfahrt« von Lord Byron.**

## Marins d'hier et d'aujourd'hui

Un port pittoresque, des habitations colorées et une vue splendide sur la mer – au premier coup d'œil, Camogli semble n'être qu'un joli village de plus sur la côte ligurienne. Mais la petite localité a une grande histoire : nommée la « ville aux mille voiles blanches » au Moyen Age en raison de sa flotte puissante, elle dénombrait encore, à la fin du XIXᵉ siècle, 500 « capitaines » pour 12 000 habitants. Des fêtes évoquent ce passé marqué par la navigation : celle du poisson, au mois de mai – au cours de laquelle le poisson est frit dans de gigantesques poêles sur la piazza – et la pro-cession navale « Stella Maris » en l'honneur de la Vierge, patronne des marins : le premier dimanche d'août, des centaines d'embarcations se dirigent vers Punta Chiappa, une bande de terre toute proche sur laquelle s'élève un autel marial. Celui qui veut voir de près les marins jeter l'ancre peut le faire du Stella Maris – l'ancien couvent surplombe les falaises et offre une vue époustouflante sur le large. Il faut toutefois réserver rapidement, car l'hôtel ne possède que douze chambres, sobres mais charmantes avec leur sol carrelé, leurs lits à baldaquin et leurs antiquités. Au restau-rant, le chef va, lui aussi, droit à l'essentiel en offrant des plats régionaux aussi simples que délicieux, servis sur la terrasse avec vue sur la mer – particulièrement belle, le soir de la procession : lorsque la nuit tombe, d'innombrables bougies flottent sur l'eau et illuminent le Golfo Paradiso.

**Livre à emporter : « Le Pèlerinage du chevalier Harold » de Lord Byron.**

| ANREISE | Camogli liegt 30 km von Genua entfernt; vom Hafen aus dauert der Bootstransfer 10 min, der Aufstieg zum Hotel über Steintreppen etwa 7 min. Mit dem Auto ist das Haus nicht erreichbar. |
| --- | --- |
| PREISE | Zimmer ab 75 €, Suite ab 115 €, inklusive Frühstück. |
| ZIMMER | 12 Zimmer. |
| KÜCHE | Ligurische Hausmannskost – ganz frisch zubereitet. |
| GESCHICHTE | Lord Byron machte das Hotel berühmt, als er 1821 hier wohnte und schrieb. Zuletzt und umfassend renoviert wurde das Haus Anfang 2009. |
| X-FAKTOR | Der verwunschene Garten. |

| ACCÈS | A 30 km de Gênes ; le transfert en bateau dure 10 min, il faut ensuite compter 7 min pour atteindre l'hôtel, inaccessible en voiture, en empruntant des escaliers de pierre. |
| --- | --- |
| PRIX | Chambre à partir de 75 €, suite à partir de 115 €, petit-déjeuner inclus. |
| CHAMBRES | 12 chambres. |
| RESTAURATION | Spécialités liguriennes à base de produits frais de saison. |
| HISTOIRE | L'hôtel doit sa célébrité à Lord Byron qui y a séjourné et travaillé en 1821. La maison a été entièrement rénovée pour la dernière fois début 2009. |
| LES « PLUS » | Le jardin enchanté. |

Ciao Bella!
Hotel Splendido, Portofino

# Hotel Splendido, Portofino

**Ciao Bella!**
All they wanted was to pray and work here, but the monks who had constructed this building high above the fishing village of Portofino in the 16th century were raided by Saracen pirates so often that they eventually fled to the hills of the hinterland. The monastery decayed – until it was converted to the summer residence of the aristocratic Baratta family and was opened by the pioneers of tourism in Portofino in 1901 as the first grand hotel in the place. Since then the opposite of monastic asceticism has prevailed at the Splendido: this hotel stands for glamour, grandeur, sensuality and style – the Italian Riviera at its very finest. Here, as a matter of course, everything blends to form a harmonious composition: from the rooms and suites, where Michel Jouannet has created a wonderful feel-good ambience in shades of cream, to the pool, which is filled with salt water instead of the standard chlorination, and the exquisite restaurant with an unforgettable sea view. Here it is nothing unusual to sit at the dinner table next to someone whose face is familiar from the cinema screen or a glossy magazine: since the Duke of Windsor was the first to sign the golden guest book, the Splendido has been a popular place to stay for celebrities. One reason for this is the service, which is both immaculate and personal. Many of the staff have worked at the hotel for decades and would do anything for the Splendido and its guests – even handle an attack by pirates.
**Books to pack: "Satura" by Eugenio Montale and "The Path to the Spiders' Nests" by Italo Calvino.**

**Hotel Splendido**
Salita Baratta 16
16034 Portofino
Italy
Tel. +39 0185 267 801
Fax +39 0185 267 806
info@splendido.net
www.hotelsplendido.com
**Open from the beginning
of April to the end of October**

| | |
|---|---|
| DIRECTIONS | 10 min walk from the village centre, 22 miles from Genoa Airport. |
| RATES | Rooms from 550 €, with sea view from 1,115 €, suites from 1,515 €, including half board. |
| ROOMS | 29 rooms and 35 suites. |
| FOOD | In addition to the Italian "La Terrazza" there is the casual "Pool Restaurant". |
| HISTORY | The hotel was thoroughly renovated in the mid-1980s and provided with a wonderful spa in the garden. |
| X-FACTOR | Yoga class in the morning with a harbour view. |

## Ciao Bella!

Sie wollten hier nur beten und arbeiten – doch die Mönche, die dieses Gebäude hoch über dem Fischerdorf Portofino im 16. Jahrhundert errichtet hatten, wurden so oft von Sarazenen-Piraten überfallen, dass sie schließlich in die Hügel des Hinterlandes flohen. Ihr Kloster verfiel – bis es zur Sommerresidenz der Adelsfamilie Baratta umgebaut und 1901 von den Tourismuspionieren Portofinos als erstes Grandhotel des Ortes eröffnet wurde. Seitdem herrscht im Haus das Gegenteil der einstigen klösterlichen Askese: Das Splendido steht für Glamour und Grandezza, Sinnlichkeit und Stil – schöner kann man die italienische Riviera nicht erleben. Hier fügt sich alles wie selbstverständlich zu einer harmonischen Komposition zusammen: von den Zimmern und Suiten, denen Michel Jouannet ein wunderbar wohltuendes Ambiente in Cremetönen verliehen hat, über den Pool, der nicht schnöde gechlort, sondern mit Salzwasser gefüllt ist, bis hin zu den erlesenen Restaurants mit unvergesslichem Blick aufs Meer. Dass am Dinnertisch nebenan jemand sitzt, dessen Gesicht man aus Kinofilmen oder Hochglanzmagazinen kennt, kann dabei durchaus vorkommen: Seit sich der Herzog von Windsor als erster Gast ins Goldene Buch eintrug, gilt das Splendido als Lieblingsadresse der Prominenz. Zu verdanken ist dies auch dem Service, der so formvollendet wie persönlich ist: Viele Mitarbeiter sind schon seit Jahrzehnten im Hotel tätig und würden für das Splendido und seine Gäste alles tun – selbst einem Piratenangriff hielten sie stand.

**Buchtipps: »Satura« von Eugenio Montale und »Wo Spinnen ihre Nester bauen« von Italo Calvino.**

## Ciao Bella !

Les moines qui ont édifié au XVI<sup>e</sup> siècle ce bâtiment surplombant le village de pêcheurs de Portofino voulaient seulement prier et travailler, mais ils furent si souvent attaqués par les Sarrasins qu'ils finirent par s'enfuir dans les collines de l'arrière-pays. Le monastère tomba en ruine, jusqu'à ce que le baron Baratta le fasse transformer en résidence d'été pour sa famille ; plus tard, en 1901, il devint le premier Grand Hôtel de Portofino. L'ascèse monacale est bien oubliée depuis : le Splendido est aujourd'hui synonyme de glamour et de grandeur, de sensualité et d'élégance – il n'y a pas de meilleur endroit pour apprécier la Riviera italienne. Ici, tout se fond naturellement en une composition harmonieuse : les chambres et les suites auxquelles Michel Jouannet a donné une ambiance aux tons crémeux, merveilleusement bienfaisante, les restaurants sélects qui offrent une vue inoubliable sur la mer, sans oublier la piscine remplie d'eau salée. Le soir, il peut très bien arriver que le visage du voisin de table nous dise quelque chose, nous l'avons vu au cinéma ou dans un magazine de luxe : le duc de Windsor a été le premier hôte à signer le livre d'or et, depuis, les personnalités se succèdent ici. Il faut dire que le personnel est aussi courtois qu'attentionné : une grande partie travaille à l'hôtel depuis des décennies et ferait tout pour le Splendido et ceux qui y séjournent – même tenir tête aux Sarrasins.

**Livres à emporter : « Satura » d'Eugenio Montale et « Le Sentier des nids d'araignée » d'Italo Calvino.**

| ANREISE | 10 min zu Fuß vom Ortskern entfernt. Die Distanz zum Flughafen Genua beträgt 37 km. |
|---|---|
| PREISE | Zimmer ab 550 €, mit Meerblick ab 1.115 €, Suite ab 1.515 €, inklusive Halbpension. |
| ZIMMER | 29 Zimmer und 35 Suiten. |
| KÜCHE | Neben dem italienischen »La Terrazza« gibt es das legere »Pool Restaurant«. |
| GESCHICHTE | Mitte der 1980er wurde das Hotel umfassend renoviert und erhielt ein herrliches Spa im Garten. |
| X-FAKTOR | Die morgendliche Yogastunde mit Blick auf den Hafen. |

| ACCÈS | Situé à 10 min à pied du centre, à 37 km de l'aéroport de Gênes. |
|---|---|
| PRIX | Chambre à partir de 550 €, avec vue sur la mer à partir de 1115 €, suite à partir de 1515 €, demi-pension incluse. |
| CHAMBRES | 29 chambres et 35 suites. |
| RESTAURATION | A côté de « La Terrazza » et ses spécialités régionales, le « Pool Restaurant » offre des collations légères. |
| HISTOIRE | L'hôtel a été complètement rénové au milieu des années 1980 et agrémenté d'un magnifique spa dans le jardin. |
| LES « PLUS » | L'heure de yoga le matin, avec vue sur le port. |

# A View of History
Torre di Bellosguardo, Firenze

# Torre di Bellosguardo, Firenze

**A View of History**

There is only one way to get out of the tourist bustle of
Florence while still enjoying all the beauty of the city: a trip
into the hills that surround the historic centre and afford a
sensational prospect of the cathedral and roofs of the city.
An elevation to the south of the Arno provides the best view,
as the name says: Bellosguardo, a place where the loveliest
postcard motifs have been photographed, where painters have
captured the panorama in oil on canvas and thinkers have
found inspiration – among them Galileo Galilei, who wrote
his "Dialogue Concerning the Two Chief World Systems"
on Bellosguardo. For a journey in time to Galileo's age and
even further back, book a room in the Torre di Bellosguardo.
A friend of Dante built the tower in the 13th century as a
hunting lodge, and during the Renaissance the Marchesi
Roti Michelozzi added a villa. Artists and aristocrats from all
over Europe have always been guests here. Between 1920
and 1940 a German baroness even established an intellectual
circle on the estate. To this day the torre has an atmosphere
of history, nobility and Bohemian life: a statue of Mercy by
Pietro Francavilla still greets visitors, frescoes by Bernardino
Poccetti adorn the lobby and the rooms are museums where
almost all the furniture derives from the former owners.
But don't get so carried away by the antique interior that
you forget to look out through the windows of the tower to
admire Florence lying at your feet.

**Book to pack: "Portrait of a Lady" by Henry James.**

| | |
|---|---|
| **Hotel Torre di Bellosguardo** | |
| Via Roti Michelozzi 2 | |
| 50124 Florence | |
| Italy | |
| Tel. +39 055 229 8145 | |
| Fax +39 055 229 008 | |
| info@torrebellosguardo.com | |
| www.torrebellosguardo.com | |
| **Open all year round** | |

| | |
|---|---|
| DIRECTIONS | About 25 min from Florence Airport. |
| RATES | Double rooms from 290 €, suites from 340 €, breakfast 20 €. |
| ROOMS | 16 rooms and suites, all individually furnished with antiques. |
| FOOD | Normally only breakfast is served. Hobby cooks can take part in outstanding cookery courses in the hotel. |
| HISTORY | In the 1980s Baron Amerigo Franchetti converted the estate into a hotel. |
| X-FACTOR | The pool – set in a wonderful Tuscan park, with a panoramic view of course. |

## Ein Blick auf die Geschichte

Um dem Touristentrubel von Florenz zu entkommen, die Stadt aber dennoch in ihrer ganzen Schönheit zu genießen, gibt es nur ein Mittel: ein Ausflug auf die Hügel, die das Zentrum umgeben und eine sensationelle Sicht über Dom und Dächer eröffnen. Eine Anhöhe im Süden des Arno bietet den besten Blick – und trägt ihn sogar im Namen: Vom Bellosguardo aus wurden die schönsten Postkartenmotive fotografiert, Maler verewigten das Panorama in Öl, Denker fanden hier Inspiration – unter ihnen Galileo Galilei, der auf dem Bellosguardo seinen »Dialog über die beiden hauptsächlichen Weltsysteme« verfasste. Wer in die Epoche Galileis und noch weiter zurück in die Geschichte reisen möchte, sollte im Torre di Bellosguardo reservieren. Ein Freund Dantes ließ den Turm im 13. Jahrhundert als Jagdschloss errichten, die Marchesi Roti Michelozzi fügten in der Renaissance eine Villa hinzu. Stets waren hier Künstler und Adlige aus ganz Europa zu Gast – zwischen 1920 und 1940 machte eine deutsche Baronin das Anwesen sogar zu einem Intellektuellenzirkel. Bis heute besitzt der Torre ein Flair von Historie, Noblesse und Boheme: So heißt noch immer eine Statue der Barmherzigkeit von Pietro Francavilla Besucher willkommen, die Lobby schmücken Fresken von Bernardino Poccetti, und die Zimmer sind Museen, in denen nahezu alle Möbel von den einstigen Eigentümern stammen. Vor lauter Begeisterung fürs antike Interieur sollte man aber nicht vergessen, aus den Turmfenstern auch hinauszuschauen – und Florenz zu bewundern, das einem zu Füßen liegt.

Buchtipp: »Bildnis einer Dame« von Henry James.

## Au fil des siècles

Pour admirer la beauté de Florence en échappant aux légions de touristes, il suffit de faire une excursion sur les collines qui l'entourent et offrent une vue sensationnelle sur le dôme et les toits. Une hauteur située au sud de l'Arno, le Bellosguardo, propose le meilleur panorama. C'est d'ici que les plus beaux motifs de cartes postales ont été photographiés, des peintres ont immortalisé la vue sur la toile, des penseurs y ont trouvé l'inspiration – c'est le cas de Galilée qui a rédigé sur le Bellosguardo son « Dialogue concernant les deux principaux systèmes du monde ». Celui qui veut faire un voyage dans le temps, jusqu'à l'époque de Galilée et plus loin encore, devrait réserver une chambre au Torre di Bellosguardo. Au XIII$^e$ siècle, un ami de Dante fit ériger la tour qui servait de pavillon de chasse, les marquis Roti Michelozzi y ajoutèrent une villa à la Renaissance. Des aristocrates et des artistes venus de toute l'Europe ont toujours été les bienvenus ici – entre 1920 et 1940, une baronne allemande fit même de la propriété un cénacle d'intellectuels. Jusqu'à ce jour, la Tour a conservé son atmosphère historique et aristocratique ainsi que son esprit bohème : ainsi, les visiteurs sont toujours accueillis par une statue de la Charité de Pietro Francavilla, le hall est agrémenté de fresques de Bernardino Poccetti et les chambres, dont presque tous les meubles proviennent des anciens propriétaires, sont de véritables musées. Mais notre admiration pour les antiquités ne devrait pas nous faire oublier de jeter un coup d'œil par la fenêtre et de contempler Florence qui s'étend à nos pieds.

Livre à emporter : « Portrait de femme » de Henry James.

| | |
|---|---|
| ANREISE | Mit dem Auto etwa 25 min vom Flughafen Florenz entfernt. |
| PREISE | Doppelzimmer ab 290 €, Suite ab 340 €, Frühstück 20 €. |
| ZIMMER | 16 Zimmer und Suiten, alle individuell mit Antiquitäten eingerichtet. |
| KÜCHE | Regulär gibt es nur Frühstück. Hobbyköche können im Hotel an ausgezeichneten Kochkursen teilnehmen. |
| GESCHICHTE | In den 1980ern verwandelte Baron Amerigo Franchetti das Anwesen in ein Hotel. |
| X-FAKTOR | Der Pool – im traumhaften toskanischen Park gelegen und natürlich mit Panoramablick. |

| | |
|---|---|
| ACCÈS | A environ 25 min en voiture de l'aéroport de Florence. |
| PRIX | Chambre double à partir de 290 €, suite à partir de 340 €, petit-déjeuner 20 €. |
| CHAMBRES | 16 chambres et suites, toutes dotées d'un ameublement ancien individuel. |
| RESTAURATION | Seul le petit-déjeuner est servi. Ceux qui le souhaitent peuvent suivre d'excellents cours de cuisine. |
| HISTOIRE | Au cours des années 1980, le baron Amerigo Franchetti a transformé la propriété en hôtel. |
| LES « PLUS » | La piscine située dans un magnifique parc toscan et qui offre naturellement une vue panoramique sur les alentours. |

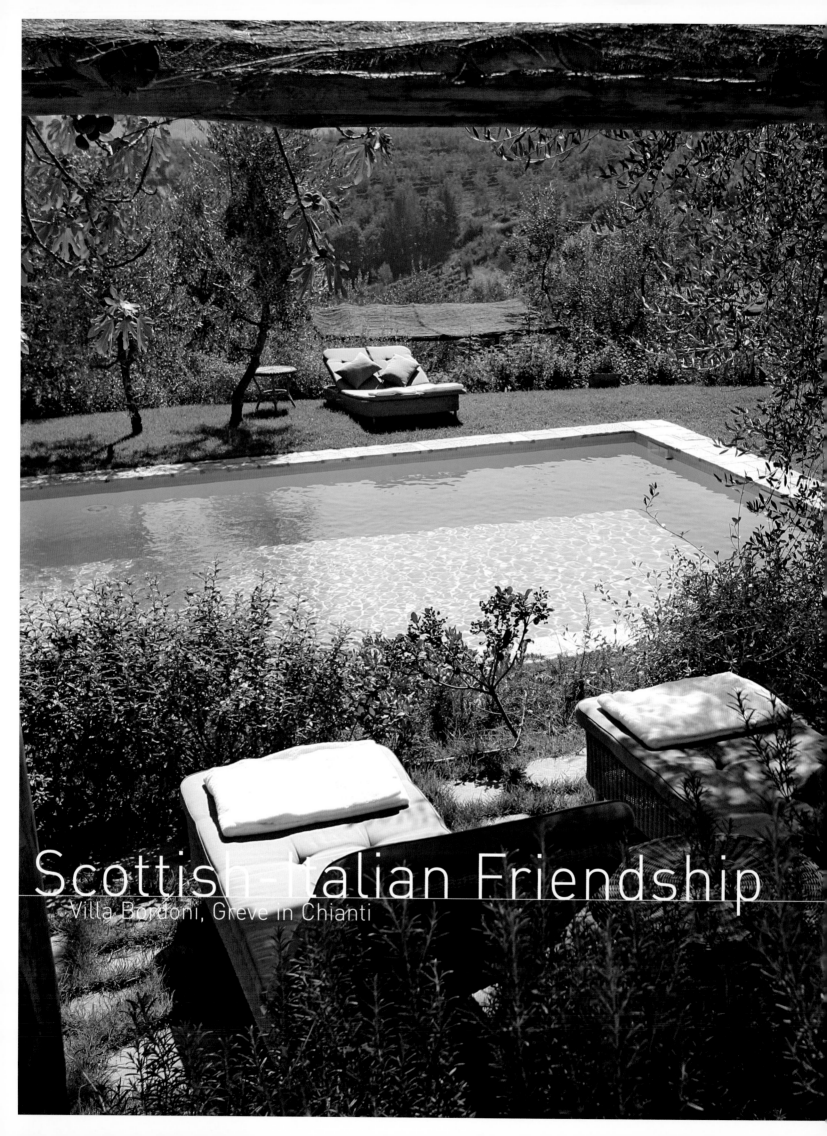

# Scottish-Italian Friendship

Villa Bordoni, Greve in Chianti

# Villa Bordoni, Greve in Chianti

**Scottish-Italian Friendship**

They exchanged the Scottish highlands for the Tuscan hills, thick tweeds for light cotton and dishes like haggis that lie heavy in the stomach for fine Mediterranean cooking: when Catherine and David Gardner left Scotland for Italy in the mid-1990s, they opened two restaurants in Florence, where the Mediterranean food on the menu was both creative and delicious, and even affordable, too. The Gardners' success with tourists and locals alike encouraged them to branch out from the restaurant business to a hotel: in the vineyards of Chianti they converted a 16th-century country house into the Villa Bordoni. With the help of the architect Andre Benaim and the designer Riccardo Barthel, the run-down estate was transformed into a guesthouse that lends a touch of elegance and extravagance to the Tuscan rustic style. The colours of each room take up the hues of the original Vietri tiles in the bathroom, rustic objects such as iron baskets or the doors of hen coops morph into lampshades or wall ornaments and curtains dyed by hand frame the windows (in order to enjoy the wonderful view, don't fail to book a room on the first floor!). The restaurant, too, is a gem, its walls adorned with a harlequin pattern of Italian vine leaves and Scottish thistles. And the Gardners' outstanding cookery courses prove to guests that not just the Scots but also travellers from all countries can master the art of Mediterranean cooking – buon appetito!

**Book to pack: "Room with a View" by E. M. Forster.**

| | |
|---|---|
| **Villa Bordoni** | |
| Via San Cresci 31/32 | |
| Località Mezzuola | |
| 50022 Greve in Chianti | |
| Italy | |
| Tel. +39 055 854 7453 and +39 055 884 0004 | |
| Fax +39 055 884 0005 | |
| info@villabordoni.com | |
| www.villabordoni.com | |
| **Open from the beginning of March to the beginning of January** | |

| | |
|---|---|
| DIRECTIONS | Above Greve in Chianti, 25 miles from Florence Airport. |
| RATES | Rooms from 170 €, suites from 260 €, including breakfast (minimum 2-night stay). |
| ROOMS | 6 rooms, 3 junior suites and 2 suites. |
| FOOD | The restaurant is open every day except Monday. In addition to lunch and dinner, sumptuous picnic baskets are available. |
| HISTORY | The estate was once the summer residence and hunting lodge of the Bordoni family, merchants from Florence. The present owners opened the villa as a hotel in 2006. |
| X-FACTOR | The panorama pool. |

## Schottisch-italienische Freundschaft

Sie tauschten die schottischen Highlands gegen die Hügel der Toskana, dicke Tweedstoffe gegen leichte Baumwolle und etwas schwer im Magen liegende Gerichte wie Haggis gegen feine Mittelmeerküche: Als Catherine und David Gardner Mitte der 1990er aus Schottland nach Italien kamen, eröffneten sie in Florenz zwei Lokale, in denen mediterrane Spezialitäten auf der Karte standen, die so kreativ wie köstlich und noch dazu erschwinglich waren. Der Erfolg, den die Gardners bei Touristen und Einheimischen hatten, gab ihnen den Mut, ihre Gastronomie durch ein Hotel zu ergänzen: In den Weinbergen des Chianti verwandelten sie einen Landsitz aus dem 16. Jahrhundert in die Villa Bordoni. Mithilfe des Architekten Andre Benaim und des Designers Riccardo Barthel wurde aus dem verfallenen Anwesen ein Gästehaus, das dem rustikalen Stil der Toskana einen Hauch Eleganz und Extravaganz verleiht. So greifen die Farben jedes Zimmers die Töne der originalen Vietri-Fliesen im Bad auf, ländliche Objekte wie Eisenkörbe oder ausrangierte Hühnerstalltüren fungieren als Lampenschirme sowie Wandornamente, und die Fenster rahmen von Hand gefärbte Vorhänge (um die wunderbare Aussicht zu genießen, unbedingt einen Raum im ersten Stock buchen!). Ein Schmuckstück ist auch das Restaurant, dessen Wände ein Harlekinmuster aus italienischen Weinblättern sowie schottischen Disteln ziert. Und dass nicht nur Schotten, sondern Reisende aller Nationen die mediterrane Küche beherrschen können, beweisen die Gardners ihren Gästen bei hervorragenden Kochkursen – buon appetito!

**Buchtipp: »Zimmer mit Aussicht« von E. M. Forster.**

## Vive l'amitié italiano-écossaise

Ils ont échangé les hauts plateaux écossais contre les collines de la Toscane, le tweed épais contre les cotonnades légères et des plats traditionnels comme le haggis contre la cuisine raffinée du Midi : arrivés en Italie au milieu des années 1990, Catherine et David Gardner ont ouvert à Florence deux restaurants proposant des spécialités méditerranéennes aussi originales que délicieuses – et, en plus, abordables. Le succès rencontré auprès des touristes et des gens du pays leur a donné des ailes et ils se sont lancés dans un projet hôtelier, transformant une propriété du XVIe siècle située dans les vignobles du Chianti en Villa Bordoni. L'architecte Andre Benaim et le designer Riccardo Barthel les ont aidés à faire du bâtiment délabré un hôtel qui apporte au style rustique de la Toscane un zeste d'élégance et d'extravagance. Ainsi, les couleurs de chaque chambre reprennent les teintes des carreaux de Vietri originaux de la salle de bains, des objets campagnards comme des corbeilles en fer forgé ou d'anciennes portes de poulailler servent d'abat-jours ou de décoration murale, et des rideaux teints à la main encadrent les fenêtres (pour bien profiter de la vue, il faut absolument prendre une chambre au premier !). Un autre petit bijou : le restaurant aux murs décorés d'un motif à carreaux associant feuilles de vignes italiennes et chardons écossais. Et, avec leurs remarquables cours de cuisine, les Gardner apportent la preuve que les Ecossais ne sont pas les seuls à maîtriser la cuisine méditerranéenne – les voyageurs de tous les pays en sont capables aussi. Buon appetito !

**Livre à emporter : « Chambre avec vue » d'E. M. Forster.**

| ANREISE | Über Greve in Chianti gelegen, 40 km vom Flughafen Florenz entfernt. |
|---|---|
| PREISE | Zimmer ab 170 €, Suite ab 260 €, inklusive Frühstück (Mindestaufenthalt 2 Nächte). |
| ZIMMER | 6 Zimmer, 3 Junior-Suiten und 2 Suiten. |
| KÜCHE | Das Restaurant ist täglich außer Montag geöffnet. Neben Lunch und Dinner bekommt man hier auch opulente Picknickkörbe. |
| GESCHICHTE | Einst war das Anwesen Sommersitz und Jagdsitz der Florentiner Kaufmannsfamilie Bordoni. Die heutigen Besitzer eröffneten die Villa 2006 als Hotel. |
| X-FAKTOR | Der Panoramapool. |

| ACCÈS | Au-dessus de Greve dans le Chianti, à 40 km de l'aéroport de Florence. |
|---|---|
| PRIX | Chambre à partir de 170 €, suite à partir de 260 €, petit-déjeuner inclus (séjour minimum 2 nuits). |
| CHAMBRES | 6 chambres, 3 junior suites et 2 suites. |
| RESTAURATION | Le restaurant est ouvert tous les jours sauf le lundi. A côté du déjeuner et du dîner, on peut commander d'opulents paniers de pique-nique. |
| HISTOIRE | Ancienne résidence estivale et pavillon de chasse des Bordoni, une famille de marchands florentins. Les propriétaires actuels ont ouvert l'hôtel en 2006. |
| LES « PLUS » | La piscine panoramique. |

# Relaxation for All the Senses

Adler Thermae, Bagno Vignoni

# Adler Thermae, Bagno Vignoni

**Relaxation for All the Senses**

3,300 feet below the earth it is warmed to 50 degrees Celsius by hot volcanic rock; it has an intense smell, as it contains not only bicarbonate but also sulphur, and it works wonders for skin irritations, painful joints and chronic bronchitis: the water of the springs at Bagno Vignoni, a tiny village south of Siena. The Etruscans and Romans knew about its healing powers, and in the 14th and 15th centuries it eased the pains of Lorenzo de' Medici, Pope Pius II and St Catherine of Siena. The pilgrimage church on the outskirts of the thermal baths, with its ancient stone pool, which seems a substitute for a piazza, is also named after her. It is one of the loveliest and most atmospheric places in Tuscany. In the nearby stone and wooden buildings the treatments are wonderfully down-to-earth and rustic – even the most impatient managers stand patiently in the queue for the legendary fango mudpacks. It is almost a pity that the thermal baths have no hotel of their own – but visitors minded to indulge themselves here for a few days will be well satisfied with the Adler Thermae resort. Constructed in what was a quarry for travertine stone, it has a view of the picture-postcard scenery of Bagno Vignoni and supplements the old healing rituals of the region with modern treatments: guests sweat in the clay steam bath of the in-house spa or the olive-wood sauna, or enjoy massages with organic cosmetic products that are based on essences of blue grapes, sheep's milk and honey.

**Book to pack: "Selected Poems" by Giosuè Carducci.**

| | |
|---|---|
| **Adler Thermae Spa Resort** | |
| San Quirico d'Orcia | |
| 53027 Bagno Vignoni | |
| Italy | |
| Tel. +39 0577 889 000 | |
| Fax +39 0577 889 999 | |
| info@adler-thermae.com | |
| www.adler-thermae.com | |
| and www.termebagnovignoni.it | |
| **Open all year round** | |

| | |
|---|---|
| DIRECTIONS | 37 and 93 miles from the airports of Siena and Florence, respectively. |
| RATES | Flat rates for a week (from 1,167 € per person) and stays of 3 or 4 days (from 587 €) can be booked. |
| ROOMS | 90 rooms and suites. |
| FOOD | Italian specialities are served in the "Cabrio" restaurant with its sliding glass roof and in the "Osteria" in the park. |
| HISTORY | The hotel was designed by architects Hugo and Hanspeter Demetz and opened in 2004. |
| X-FACTOR | Even if you are here to improve your health, the Tuscan wines from the travertine cellar are a rewarding sin to commit. |

## Mit allen Sinnen entspannen

Es wird tausend Meter unter der Erde von heißem Vulkan-
gestein auf 50 Grad Celsius erwärmt, riecht etwas intensiver,
da es neben Bikarbonat auch Schwefel enthält, und wirkt
Wunder bei gereizter Haut, schmerzenden Gelenken sowie
chronischer Bronchitis: das Quellwasser von Bagno Vignoni,
einem winzigen Dorf südlich von Siena. Schon die Etrusker
und Römer kannten seine wohltuende Kraft, und im 14. und
15. Jahrhundert linderte es die Leiden von Lorenzo de' Medici,
Papst Pius II. und der Heiligen Katharina von Siena. Nach
ihr ist auch die Wallfahrtskirche am Rande des Thermalbades
mit seinem antiken Steinbecken benannt, das einst mitten
im Ort erbaut wurde und die Piazza zu ersetzen scheint – es
ist einer der schönsten und stimmungsvollsten Plätze der
Toskana. In den umliegenden Gebäuden aus Stein und Holz
kurt man wunderbar rustikal und bodenständig; für die
sagenhaften Fango-Packungen stehen selbst die nervösesten
Manager geduldig Schlange. Es ist fast schade, dass die
Therme kein eigenes Hotel besitzt – doch wer sich hier
mehrere Tage lang Gutes tun möchte, ist im nahen Resort
Adler Thermae bestens aufgehoben. In einem ehemaligen
Travertinsteinbruch errichtet, blickt es auf die Bilderbuch-
landschaft von Bagno Vignoni und ergänzt die alten Heil-
rituale der Region um moderne Anwendungen: Im Spa des
Hauses schwitzen Gäste im Tonerde-Dampfbad oder in der
Olivenholz-Sauna und lassen sich mit Bio-Kosmetikprodukten
massieren, die auf Essenzen von blauen Weintrauben,
Schafsmilch oder Honig basieren.
**Buchtipp: »Ça ira. Zwölf Sonette« von Giosuè Carducci.**

## Détente et bien-être

L'eau de la source de Bagno Vignoni, un minuscule village
au sud de Sienne, est réchauffée mille mètres sous terre par
la pierre volcanique chaude. Elle atteint une température de
50 degrés Celsius, contient du bicarbonate et du soufre, ce
qui lui donne une certaine odeur. Ses effets sont merveilleux
en cas d'irritation cutanée, d'articulations douloureuses et
de bronchite chronique. Les Etrusques et les Romains
connaissaient déjà ses propriétés bienfaisantes et, au XIVe
et au XVe siècle, elle soulageait les douleurs de Laurent de
Médicis, du pape Pie II et de sainte Catherine de Sienne.
L'église de pèlerinage édifiée au bord du bain thermal, avec
son bassin de pierre construit autrefois au milieu du village
et qui semble remplacer la piazza, lui doit aussi son nom
– c'est l'un des plus beaux endroits de la Toscane et il y
règne une atmosphère particulière. Dans les bâtiments de
pierre et de bois qui l'entourent, on peut faire des cures
merveilleusement rustiques et simples ; même les managers
les plus nerveux font la queue pour profiter des bienfaits
d'un bain de boue. Les bains thermaux n'ont pas d'hôtel,
c'est presque dommage, mais celui qui veut se faire du bien
ici, pendant quelques jours, se sentira on ne peut mieux au
Resort Adler Thermae tout proche. Construit dans une
ancienne carrière de travertin, il domine le paysage idyllique
de Bagno Vignoni et les soins modernes qu'il offre complètent
les anciens rituels de guérison : dans le spa, les hôtes peuvent
transpirer dans un bain de vapeur étrusque en terre glaise ou
dans le sauna en bois d'olivier. Ils peuvent se faire masser
avec des produits cosmétiques bio basés sur des essences
de vigne rouge, du lait de brebis et du miel.
**Livre à emporter : « Ça ira » de Giosuè Carducci.**

| | |
|---|---|
| ANREISE | 60 bzw. 150 km von den Flughäfen Siena und Florenz entfernt. |
| PREISE | Buchbar sind Wochenpauschalen (ab 1.167 € pro Person) und 3- oder 4-Tage-Aufenthalte (ab 587 €). |
| ZIMMER | 90 Zimmer und Suiten. |
| KÜCHE | Im »Cabrio«-Restaurant mit beweglichem Glasdach und in der »Osteria« im Park werden italienische Spezialitäten serviert. |
| GESCHICHTE | Das Hotel wurde von den Architekten Hugo und Hanspeter Demetz entworfen und eröffnete 2004. |
| X-FAKTOR | Auch wer hier kurt und entschlackt: Die toskanischen Weine aus dem Travertinkeller sind eine Sünde wert. |

| | |
|---|---|
| ACCÈS | A 60 km/150 km des aéroports de Sienne et de Florence. |
| PRIX | Forfait hebdomadaire à partir de 1167 € par personne et séjour de 3 ou 4 jours à partir de 587 €. |
| CHAMBRES | 90 chambres et suites. |
| RESTAURATION | Spécialités italiennes au « Cabrio », doté d'un toit ouvrant en verre, et à l'« Osteria » du parc. |
| HISTOIRE | Conçu par les architectes Hugo et Hanspeter Demetz, l'hôtel a ouvert ses portes en 2004. |
| LES « PLUS » | Eliminer les toxines est une bonne chose, mais pas de santé sans plaisir : les vins toscans conservés dans la cave en travertin valent le détour. |

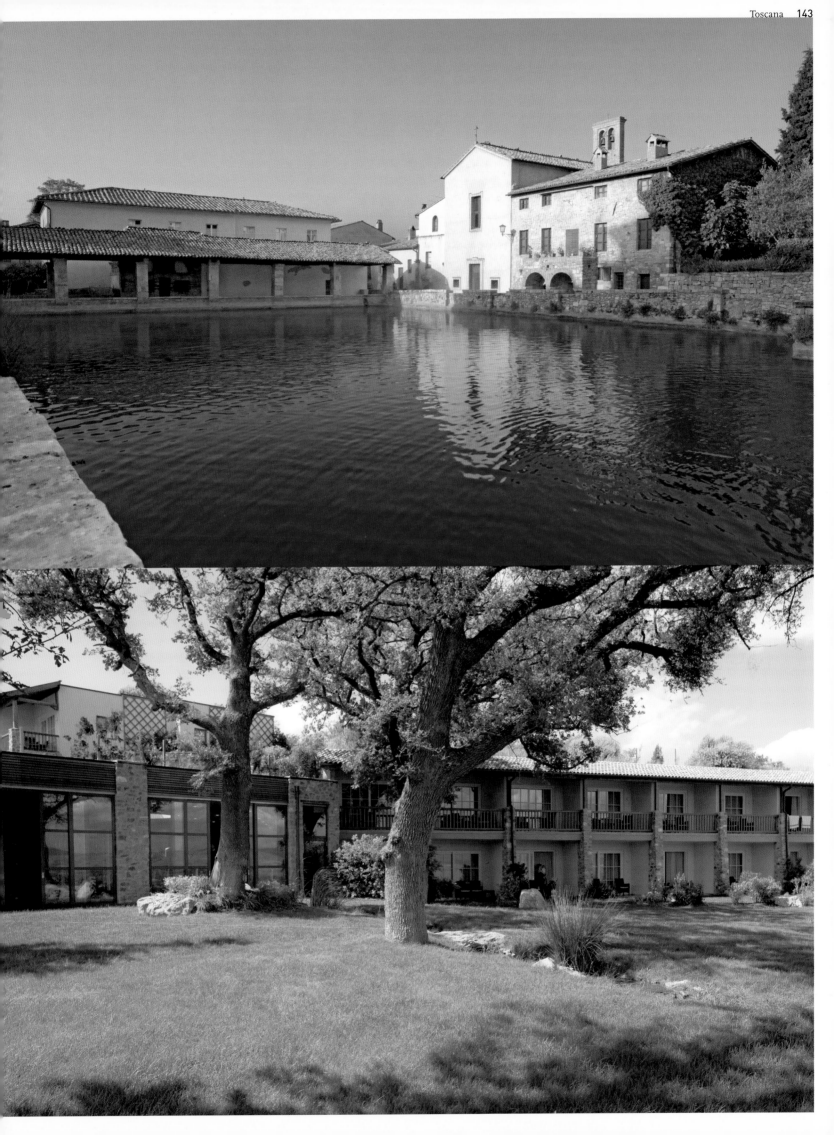

# A Private Stay in Tuscany
Castello di Vicarello, near Siena

# Castello di Vicarello, near Siena

**A Private Stay in Tuscany**

The Maremma is the other face of Tuscany: away from the rolling hills, picturesque villages and cities of art, Tuscany is less spectacular and more authentic, with a raw beauty that visitors passing through often fail to notice. But those who do take note sense something wild and romantic, perhaps familiar from the Camargue, or something melancholy, as on the Peloponnese out of season – and they fall in love with it. This is what happened to Carlo and Aurora Baccheschi Berti. They had seen the world and worked for many years on Bali as textile designers before discovering a tumbledown castle in the Maremma – and the magic of the place. They restored Castello di Vicarello energetically and stylishly, and turned it into a hotel that exudes the rustic charm of the region and at the same time lends it a touch of Bohemian atmosphere, a hotel that is run like a private home and, wonderfully, attracts just the right clientele: people who travel often and in style, and are as happy to talk about this as they are to hear the stories of like-minded guests. The best part of a stay is dinner, sitting at a long table, or relaxing together by the pools. For the necessary bit of privacy there are six rooms and a villa furnished with antiques, art books and some open fireplaces. Hotel guests have to do without extras such as television – but who needs a screen with pictures from round the world when the natural images of the Maremma are right outside?

**Book to pack: "Under the Tuscan Sun" by Frances Mayes.**

| | |
|---|---|
| **Castello di Vicarello**<br>58044 Poggi del Sasso<br>Cinigiano<br>Italy<br>Tel. +39 0564 990 718 and +39 0564 990 447<br>Fax +39 0564 990 718<br>info@vicarello.it<br>www.vicarello.it<br>**Open all year round** | **DIRECTIONS** In southern Tuscany, 87 and 130 miles from Florence and Rome airports, respectively.<br>**RATES** Rooms from 370 €, suites from 580 €, villa from 1,100 €, including breakfast.<br>**ROOMS** 1 double room and 6 suites.<br>**FOOD** Fruit and vegetables are grown in the hotel garden, game is shot locally; Aurora reveals her best recipes in cookery courses.<br>**HISTORY** Castello di Vicarello dates from the 12th century and was opened as a guesthouse in 2003.<br>**X-FACTOR** Ayurveda treatments in the spa. |

## Die Toskana ganz privat

In der Maremma zeigt die Toskana ihr zweites Gesicht: Abseits der sanften Hügel, der pittoresken Dörfer und berühmten Kunststädte gibt sie sich hier unspektakulärer und ursprünglicher; von einer rauen Schönheit, an der manche Besucher achtlos vorüberfahren. Doch wer sie bemerkt, spürt etwas Wildromantisches, das er vielleicht aus der Camargue kennt, etwas Melancholisches, wie es der Peloponnes außerhalb der Saison besitzt – und er verliebt sich in sie. So ging es auch Carlo und Aurora Baccheschi Berti. Sie hatten die Welt gesehen und lange Jahre auf Bali als Textildesigner gearbeitet, ehe sie in der Maremma eine verfallene Burg entdeckten – und mit ihr ihre Magie. Sie restaurierten das Castello di Vicarello mit so viel Energie wie Stil und verwandelten es in ein Hotel, das den rustikalen Charme der Region verströmt und ihm zugleich einen Hauch Boheme verleiht, das wie ein Privathaus geführt wird und wunderbarerweise die exakt passende Klientel anzieht: Menschen, die oft und gepflegt reisen und gerne davon erzählen, genauso wie sie neugierig auf die Geschichten Gleichgesinnter sind. Am schönsten sitzt man beim Dinner an der langen Tafel zusammen oder entspannt gemeinsam an den Pools. Für das nötige Quäntchen Privatsphäre sorgen die sechs Zimmer sowie eine Villa, die mit Antiquitäten, Kunstbüchern und zum Teil offenen Kaminen ausgestattet sind. Auf Extras wie einen Fernseher muss man verzichten – doch wer braucht schon flimmernde Bilder aus aller Welt, wenn er die natürlichen der Maremma direkt vor der Tür hat?
Buchtipp: »Unter der Sonne der Toskana« von Frances Mayes.

## La Toscane en privé

C'est dans la Maremme que la Toscane montre son autre visage : à l'écart des collines aux formes douces, des villages pittoresques et des villes au riche patrimoine artistique, elle est moins spectaculaire et plus authentique, d'une beauté rude que l'on peut méconnaître. Mais celui qui la remarque y discerne un romantisme sauvage qu'il a peut-être déjà rencontré en Camargue, quelque chose de mélancolique que possède aussi le Péloponnèse hors-saison – et il en tombe amoureux. C'est ce qui est arrivé à Carlo et Aurora Baccheschi Berti. Ils avaient vu le monde et travaillé de longues années à Bali comme designers textiles, lorsqu'ils découvrirent un château fort en ruine dans la Maremme et la magie des lieux. Ils ont restauré le Castello di Vicarello avec autant d'énergie que d'élégance et l'ont transformé en un hôtel qui possède le charme rustique de la région, mais avec un accent bohème. Il est dirigé comme une maison particulière et attire miraculeusement la clientèle adéquate : des gens qui voyagent souvent, recherchent le raffinement, et aiment autant raconter leurs passions qu'écouter les récits de ceux qui partagent leurs idées. Le soir, pour dîner, la longue table accueille tous les hôtes et il est bon aussi de se détendre ensemble au bord de la piscine. L'intimité nécessaire est assurée par les chambres et la villa, en partie dotées de cheminées et décorées d'antiquités et de livres d'art. Il faut renoncer à la télévision – mais qui a besoin de voir des images du monde sur un écran quand le paysage de la Maremme est devant sa porte ?
Livre à emporter : « Sous le Soleil de Toscane » de Frances Mayes.

| ANREISE | In der südlichen Toskana gelegen, 140 bzw. 210 km von den Flughäfen Florenz und Rom entfernt. |
| --- | --- |
| PREISE | Zimmer ab 370 €, Suite ab 580 €, Villa ab 1.100 €, inklusive Frühstück. |
| ZIMMER | 1 Zimmer und 6 Suiten. |
| KÜCHE | Obst und Gemüse gedeihen im eigenen Garten, Wild ist selbst gejagt. Ihre besten Rezepte verrät Aurora in Kochkursen. |
| GESCHICHTE | Das Castello di Vicarello stammt aus dem 12. Jahrhundert, es wurde 2003 als Gästehaus eröffnet. |
| X-FAKTOR | Die Ayurveda-Behandlungen im Spa. |

| ACCÈS | Dans le sud de la Toscane, à 140 km de l'aéroport de Florence, à 210 km de l'aéroport de Rome. |
| --- | --- |
| PRIX | Chambre à partir de 370 €, suite à partir de 580 €, villa à partir de 1100 €, petit-déjeuner inclus. |
| CHAMBRES | 1 chambres et 6 suites. |
| RESTAURATION | Fruits et légumes du jardin, gibier chassé ici-même. La maîtresse de maison révèle ses meilleures recettes dans des cours de cuisine. |
| HISTOIRE | Le Castello di Vicarello date du XIIe siècle, l'hôtel a été ouvert en 2003. |
| LES « PLUS » | Cure spa avec traitements ayurvédiques. |

# A Declaration of Love
Il Pellicano, Porto Ercole

# Il Pellicano, Porto Ercole

**A Declaration of Love**

He was a British pilot who came to fame when he jumped out of his crashing plane without a parachute and survived. She was an American socialite who looked a little like Grace Kelly and had an affair with Clark Gable. When Michael Graham and Patsy Daszel met at Pelican Point in California, it was love at first sight. Together the couple moved to Italy and fell in love all over again – with a plot of land on the rocky coast of Monte Argentario, which was once an island and is now connected to the mainland of the Maremma. They built themselves a home there high above the Mediterranean in 1965 and named it "Il Pellicano" after the place where they met. Their private paradise quickly became a destination for the jet set – the Grahams invited Ted Kennedy to stay, lay in the sun with Charlie Chaplin and clinked glasses with Gianni Agnelli. When they returned to America they sold the estate to a friend, who converted it into a public hotel. Since then guests have been able to enjoy a holiday as stylish and sophisticated as the first glamorous residents. The best accommodation is in the cottages that are situated highest up (don't fail to book a room with a sea view). By day guests swim in the seawater pool and in the evening enjoy Michelin-starred dishes. The spa, newly renovated in the style of a beach house, is truly wonderful. What a pity Michael Graham and Patsy Daszel never saw it – it would have been love at first sight once more.

**Book to pack: "The Divine Comedy" by Dante Alighieri.**

**Il Pellicano Hotel**
Località Sbarcatello
58018 Porto Ercole
Italy
Tel. +39 0564 858 111
Fax +39 0564 833 418
info@pellicanohotel.com
www.pellicanohotel.com
**Open from the beginning
of April to the end of October**

| | |
|---|---|
| DIRECTIONS | On the south coast of Monte Argentario, 93 miles from Rome Airport. |
| RATES | Rooms from 420 €, suites from 750 €, including breakfast. |
| ROOMS | 35 rooms and 15 suites. |
| FOOD | In addition to the main restaurant, "all'Aperto" serves Tuscan cuisine under the stars. |
| HISTORY | Il Pellicano was completed in 1965 as a private home; Roberto Sciò bought it in 1979; it is a member of Relais & Châteaux. |
| X-FACTOR | The gardens by landscape architect Paolo Pejrone and the private rocky beach. |

## Eine Liebeserklärung

Er war ein britischer Pilot, der berühmt wurde, als er bei einem Absturz seiner Maschine ohne Fallschirm aus dem Flugzeug sprang und überlebte. Sie war eine amerikanische Socialite, die ein bisschen an Grace Kelly erinnerte und eine Liaison mit Clark Gable hatte: Als sich Michael Graham und Patsy Daszel am Pelican Point in Kalifornien trafen, war es »love at first sight«. Gemeinsam zog das Paar nach Italien und verliebte sich dort erneut – in ein Grundstück an der Felsenküste des Monte Argentario, einer ehemaligen Insel, die heute mit dem Festland der Maremma verbunden ist. Hoch über dem Mittelmeer bauten sie dort 1965 ihre Residenz und tauften sie nach dem Ort ihres Kennenlernens »Il Pellicano«. Aus dem persönlichen Paradies wurde schnell ein Lieblingsziel des Jetsets – die Grahams hatten Ted Kennedy zu Gast, lagen mit Charlie Chaplin in der Sonne und stießen mit Gianni Agnelli aufs Leben an. Als sie nach Amerika zurückkehrten, verkauften sie das Anwesen an einen Freund, der es in ein öffentliches Hotel verwandelte – seitdem kann man hier so stilvoll und sophisticated urlauben wie einst die glamourösen Bewohner. Am besten wohnt man in den höchstgelegenen Cottages (unbedingt ein Zimmer mit Meerblick buchen!), genießt tagsüber den Salzwasserpool und abends Menüs, die mit einem Michelin-Stern gekrönt sind. Ganz fabelhaft ist das im Stil eines Strandhauses neu renovierte Spa; fast schade, dass Michael Graham und Patsy Daszel es nicht mehr erlebt haben – es wäre ein weiteres Mal Liebe auf den ersten Blick gewesen.

**Buchtipp: »Die Göttliche Komödie« von Dante Alighieri.**

## Déclaration d'amour

Il était une fois un pilote britannique rescapé d'un crash – il avait sauté sans parachute, ce qui le rendit célèbre. Elle était une héritière américaine, ressemblait un peu à Grace Kelly et avait eu une liaison avec Clark Gable : le jour où Michael Graham et Patsy Daszel firent connaissance à Pelican Point en Californie, ce fut le coup de foudre. Partis s'installer en Italie, ils tomberont à nouveau amoureux, cette fois d'un terrain sur la falaise escarpée du Monte Argentario, une ancienne île reliée aujourd'hui à la Maremme. Ils y construiront en 1965 leur résidence qui surplombe la Méditerranée et la baptiseront « Il Pellicano », en souvenir de leur première rencontre. Ils accueillirent bientôt leurs amis de la jet-set dans leur paradis personnel – invitant Ted Kennedy, se reposant au soleil avec Charlie Chaplin et trinquant avec Gianni Agnelli. Lorsqu'ils retournèrent aux Etats-Unis, les Graham vendirent la propriété à un ami qui la transforma en hôtel. Depuis, on peut passer ici des vacances aussi élégantes et sophistiquées que les hôtes glamour d'autrefois. Pour vivre des moments parfaits, il faut séjourner dans l'un des cottages situés en hauteur (réserver absolument une chambre avec vue sur la mer), se détendre pendant la journée dans la piscine d'eau salée et savourer, le soir, les menus du restaurant pourvu d'une étoile au Michelin. Le spa rénové dans le style d'une maison de plage est fabuleux ; dommage que Michael Graham et Patsy Daszel ne l'aient pas connu, ils auraient craqué une fois de plus, c'est sûr.

**Livre à emporter : « La Divine Comédie » de Dante Alighieri.**

| | |
|---|---|
| ANREISE | An der Südostküste des Monte Argentario gelegen, 150 km vom Flughafen Rom entfernt. |
| PREISE | Zimmer ab 420 €, Suite ab 750 €, inklusive Frühstück. |
| ZIMMER | 35 Zimmer und 15 Suiten. |
| KÜCHE | Neben dem Hauptrestaurant gibt es das toskanische »all'Aperto« unter freiem Himmel. |
| GESCHICHTE | Als Privathaus wurde Il Pellicano 1965 eröffnet; Roberto Sciò erwarb es 1979. Es ist Mitglied bei Relais & Châteaux. |
| X-FAKTOR | Die Gärten des Landschaftsarchitekten Paolo Pejrone und der private Felsenstrand. |

| | |
|---|---|
| ACCÈS | Sur la côte sud-est du Monte Argentario, à 150 km de l'aéroport de Rome. |
| PRIX | Chambre à partir de 420 €, suite à partir de 750 €, petit-déjeuner inclus. |
| CHAMBRES | 35 chambres et 15 suites. |
| RESTAURATION | A côté du restaurant principal, l'« all'Aperto » toscan. |
| HISTOIRE | La résidence Il Pellicano date de 1965 ; Roberto Sciò l'a achetée en 1979. L'hôtel est membre de Relais & Châteaux. |
| LES « PLUS » | Les jardins de l'architecte paysagiste Paolo Pejrone et la plage rocheuse privée. |

# A Hotel like a Painting
Palazzo Terranova, near Perugia

# Palazzo Terranova, near Perugia

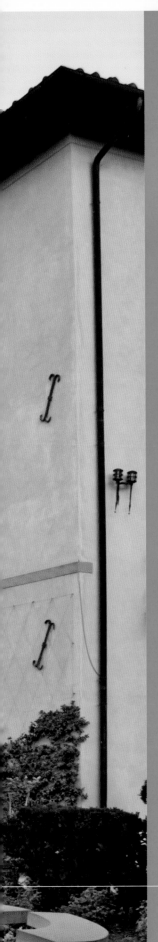

**A Hotel like a Painting**

Piero della Francesco was an early Renaissance master. No other painter of the time could lend such a tender look to a Madonna. His unusually light colours made it seem as if the scenes in his pictures were being played out beneath the midday sun, and thanks to his frescoes the Cappella Bacci in the Basilica di San Francesco of Arezzo gained fame as the "Sistine Chapel of Tuscany". Twenty-five miles south-east of Arezzo in the hills of Umbria, Palazzo Terranova is inspired by the characteristic colours of Piero della Francesco. In refined dove grey, delicate peach yellow or washed-out sky blue, strong tones of terracotta, glowing crystal green or an almost daring raspberry pink – every room in the hotel is painted in a different shade and designed in the luxurious Italian country-house style (the fact that English accessories pop up here and there is because the former owner was an Englishwoman). Guests can sleep in outsize four-poster beds, bathe in hand-made marble tubs and with a little luck have an open fireplace, a private walnut-wood library stocked with classics or a little balcony with a view of the austere landscape. It's almost too much of a good thing that the rooms of the palazzo are named after Italian operas or opera characters. Luckily Piero della Francesco was not thought to be a vain artist – he would hardly have regarded Trovatore and the rooms named after other singers as rivals to his art.

**Book to pack: "Mistero Buffo" by Dario Fo.**

| | |
|---|---|
| **Palazzo Terranova** | **DIRECTIONS** 84 and 155 miles from Florence and Rome airports, respectively. |
| Località Ronti | **RATES** Rooms from 305 €, villa from 840 €, including breakfast. |
| 06010 Morra, Città di Castello | **ROOMS** 8 rooms and 1 villa (for max. 5 guests). |
| Italy | **FOOD** The restaurant serves Umbrian specialities and Italian classics – the pizza and focaccia from the wood-fired oven are made with guests' choice of toppings. |
| Tel. +39 075 857 0083 | |
| Fax +39 075 857 0014 | |
| info@palazzoterranova.com | **HISTORY** The late 17th-century palazzo opened as a hotel in 1997. |
| www.palazzoterranova.com | **X-FACTOR** The pool and spa are small but exclusive. |
| **Open from March to November** | |

## Ein Hotel wie gemalt

Piero della Francesca war ein Meister der Frührenaissance:
Kein anderer Maler seiner Zeit konnte einer Madonnenfigur
einen so zärtlichen Blick geben wie er, seine ungewöhnlich
hellen Töne ließen seine Bilder wirken, als spielten ihre
Szenen unter der Mittagssonne, und dank seiner Fresken
wurde die Cappella Bacci in der Basilica di San Francesco
von Arezzo als »Sixtinische Kapelle der Toskana« berühmt.
Von den charakteristischen Farben, mit denen Piero della
Francesca arbeitete, ist der Palazzo Terranova inspiriert
– vierzig Kilometer südöstlich von Arezzo in den Hügeln
Umbriens gelegen. Ob in edlem Taubengrau, zartem
Pfirsichgelb oder verwaschenem Himmelblau, kräftigen
Terrakottatönen, leuchtendem Kristallgrün oder fast gewag-
tem Himbeerpink – jeder Raum des Hotels ist unterschied-
lich gestrichen und im luxuriösen italienischen Landhausstil
gestaltet (dass hier und da auch ein englisches Accessoire
aufblitzt, liegt daran, dass die ehemalige Besitzerin Britin
war). Man kann in extragroßen Himmelbetten schlafen, in
handgefertigten Marmorwannen baden und besitzt mit etwas
Glück einen offenen Kamin, eine mit Klassikern gefüllte
Privatbibliothek aus Walnussholz oder ein Balkönchen mit
Blick über die herbe Landschaft. Es ist beinahe zu viel des
Guten, dass die Zimmer des Palazzo auch noch nach italie-
nischen Opern oder Opercharakteren benannt wurden.
Doch glücklicherweise galt Piero della Francesca als uneitler
Künstler – er hätte im »Trovatore« und seinen Sänger-
kollegen wohl keine Konkurrenz gesehen.
Buchtipp: »Obszöne Fabeln. Mistero Buffo: Szenische
Monologe« von Dario Fo.

## Peinture et musique

Piero della Francesca était un maître du début de la
Renaissance : aucun autre peintre de son temps ne sut
donner un regard aussi tendre à la Vierge, sa palette inhabi-
tuellement claire éveillait chez le spectateur l'impression
que ses scènes se passaient sous le soleil de midi, et c'est
grâce à ses fresques que la chapelle Bacci de la basilique di
San Francesco d'Arezzo est devenue célèbre sous le nom de
« chapelle Sixtine de la Toscane ». Situé à 40 kilomètres au
sud-est d'Arezzo dans les collines d'Ombrie, le Palazzo
Teranova montre des couleurs sorties tout droit des tableaux
de Piero della Francesca. Noble gris perle, délicat jaune pêche
ou bleu ciel délavé, tons puissants de terre cuite, vert cristallin
éclatant, ou rose framboise écrasée, chaque pièce de l'hôtel
est peinte d'une couleur différente et aménagée dans le style
luxueux des maisons de campagne italiennes (si un accessoire
anglais apparaît ici et là, c'est que l'ancienne propriétaire était
britannique). On peut dormir dans d'immenses lits à baldaquin, se baigner dans des bassins en marbre fabriqués à la
main et, avec un peu de chance, disposer d'une cheminée,
d'une bibliothèque en noyer remplie de grands classiques
ou d'un petit balcon avec vue sur le paysage. Et la cerise sur
le gâteau : les noms des chambres sont issus du monde de
l'opéra italien. Cela n'aurait probablement pas dérangé Piero
della Francesca qui n'était pas prétentieux dit-on – il n'aurait
sans doute pas considéré Le Trouvère et Rigoletto comme
des rivaux.
Livre à emporter : « Mystère bouffe : Jonglerie populaire »
de Dario Fo.

| ANREISE | 135 bzw. 250 km von den Flughäfen Florenz und Rom entfernt. |
| --- | --- |
| PREISE | Zimmer ab 305 €, Villa ab 840 €, inklusive Frühstück. |
| ZIMMER | 8 Zimmer sowie 1 Villa (diese für max. 5 Gäste). |
| KÜCHE | Das Restaurant serviert Spezialitäten aus Umbrien und italienische Klassiker – die Pizza und Focaccia aus dem Holzofen werden nach Wunsch belegt. |
| GESCHICHTE | Der Palazzo aus dem späten 17. Jahrhundert wurde 1997 als Hotel eröffnet. |
| X-FAKTOR | Pool und Spa sind klein, aber fein. |

| ACCÈS | A 135 km de l'aéroport de Florence, à 250 km de celui de Rome. |
| --- | --- |
| PRIX | Chambre à partir de 305 €, villa à partir de 840 €, petit-déjeuner inclus. |
| CHAMBRES | 8 chambres et 1 villa, celle-ci pouvant accueillir 5 personnes maximum. |
| RESTAURATION | Spécialités d'Ombrie et classiques de la cuisine italienne au restaurant – la pizza et la focaccia cuites au four à bois sont garnies selon vos désirs. |
| HISTOIRE | Abrité dans un palais du XVIIe siècle, l'hôtel a ouvert ses portes en 1997. |
| LES « PLUS » | Dispose d'une piscine et d'un spa, petits mais sympas. |

# Love at Second Sight

Locanda del Gallo, Gubbio

# Locanda del Gallo, Gubbio

**Love at Second Sight**

No, Umbria is not a great beauty, no star in the spotlight. This relatively bleak and thinly populated region at the heart of Italy, the only region in the country that has neither a coast nor a border to a neighbouring country, has always kept a low profile. Pilgrims and conquerors on the way to Rome used simply to pass through, and for many tourists today Umbria is just a place to stop over. However, it is possible to make history even in the shadow of the Eternal City and Tuscany, to be influential even from behind the scenes. To learn that Umbria has produced great men such as the Renaissance painter Raphael, possesses one of Europe's most important places of pilgrimage, in Assisi, and produces exquisite ceramics and wonderfully soft cashmere wool in Deruta and Solomeo comes as a surprise to many travellers – and is a good reason to spend more time here. Locanda del Gallo is a wonderful base for making excursions. Like the landscape itself, it has an unassuming appearance and reveals unexpected details only at a second glance. The simple rooms are equipped with furniture from the Far East that the owners brought back from many journeys, and in the restaurant oriental spices add refinement to the Mediterranean food. Those who like to take a look behind the scenes should ask Paola and Irish for their advice on sightseeing, and complement a trip to the cities of art with a course in weaving or cookery to round off a journey of discovery in Italy.

**Book to pack: "Wind Shift" by Andrea De Carlo.**

| | |
|---|---|
| **Locanda del Gallo** | |
| Località Santa Cristina | |
| 06020 Gubbio | |
| Italy | |
| Tel./Fax +39 075 922 9912 | |
| info@locandadelgallo.it | |
| www.locandadelgallo.it | |
| **Open all year round** | |

| | |
|---|---|
| DIRECTIONS | Between Gubbio and Perugia, 105 and 144 miles from Florence and Rome airports, respectively. |
| RATES | Rooms from 70 €, including breakfast. |
| ROOMS | 10 rooms (no air conditioning or TV). |
| FOOD | The vegetables are grown on the grounds, and the owners press their own olive oil. |
| HISTORY | The land once belonged to the del Grillo family, Florentine nobles who built a palazzo here in the 17th century. Locanda del Gallo was erected on the palazzo ruins in 1995. |
| X-FACTOR | The saltwater pool in the garden. |

## Liebe auf den zweiten Blick

Nein, eine Schönheit, ein Star im Rampenlicht ist Umbrien
nicht. Die vergleichsweise raue und dünn besiedelte Region
im Herzen Italiens (übrigens die einzige des Landes, die
weder eine Meeresküste noch eine Grenze zum Ausland
besitzt) wirkt seit jeher ein bisschen unscheinbar – für
Pilger und Eroberer auf dem Weg nach Rom war sie früher
nur Durchgangsstation, für viele Touristen ist sie heute
lediglich Zwischenstopp. Doch selbst im Schatten der
Ewigen Stadt und der Toskana lässt sich Geschichte schrei-
ben, selbst aus der zweiten Reihe lassen sich Fäden ziehen:
Dass Umbrien große Söhne wie den Renaissance-Meister
Raffael hervorgebracht hat, mit Assisi eine der wichtigsten
Wallfahrtsstätten Europas besitzt, in Deruta und Solomeo
die edelste Keramikware und die weichste Kaschmirwolle
produziert werden, ist für so manchen Reisenden eine
Überraschung – und Grund, sich hier mehr Zeit zu nehmen.
Ein wunderbarer Ausgangspunkt für Ausflüge ist die Locanda
del Gallo, die sich ganz wie das Land zunächst unaufgeregt
zeigt und erst auf den zweiten Blick unerwartete Details
freigibt. So stehen in den schlichten Zimmern Möbelstücke
aus dem Fernen Osten, welche die Besitzer von zahlreichen
Reisen mitgebracht haben, und im Restaurant werden
mediterrane Menüs mit orientalischen Gewürzen verfeinert.
Wer an den Blicken hinter die Kulissen Gefallen findet, sollte
sich von Paola und Irish auch beim Sightseeing beraten
lassen und neben den Kunststädten einen Weberei- oder
Kochkurs aufs Programm setzen, der die italienische
Entdeckungsreise komplett macht.

**Buchtipp: »Wenn der Wind dreht« von Andrea De Carlo.**

## Le second regard

Non, l'Ombrie n'est pas une beauté, une star sous le feu des
projecteurs. Rude et peu habitée, cette région située au cœur
de la péninsule italienne – elle est la seule à ne pas être
baignée par la mer et à ne pas avoir de frontière avec un
autre pays – a toujours semblé plutôt insignifiante. Autrefois,
les pèlerins et les conquérants en route vers Rome n'y res-
taient que le temps d'une brève station, de nombreux touristes
aujourd'hui se contentent d'y faire étape. Pourtant, la Ville
éternelle et la Toscane n'ont pas la prérogative de l'Histoire
– il ne fallait pas être aux premières loges pour tirer les
ficelles – et bien des voyageurs sont surpris d'apprendre que
Raphaël, maître de la Renaissance, était un enfant du pays,
qu'Assise, un des lieux de pèlerinage majeurs en Europe,
est située en Ombrie, que la céramique la plus fine et le
cachemire le plus soyeux sont produits à Deruta et Solomeo
– raison de plus pour prendre son temps ici. Un merveilleux
point de départ pour apprendre à connaître la région est la
Locanda del Gallo qui, à l'instar du paysage, semble discrète
et ne montre qu'au second coup d'œil des détails inattendus.
Ainsi, les chambres sobres abritent des meubles originaires
d'Extrême-Orient que les propriétaires ont rapportés de leurs
nombreux voyages et, au restaurant, la cuisine méditerranéenne est enrichie d'épices orientales. Celui qui s'intéresse
à l'envers du décor devrait chercher conseil auprès de Paola
et Irish et mettre au programme, à côté de la visite des villes
d'art, un cours de tissage ou de cuisine qui complète la
découverte de l'Italie.

**Livre à emporter : « Week-end à Moulin-Vent » d'Andrea
De Carlo.**

| | | | | |
|---|---|---|---|---|
| ANREISE | Zwischen Gubbio und Perugia gelegen, 170 bzw. 230 km von den Flughäfen Florenz und Rom entfernt. | ACCÈS | Entre Gubbio et Pérouse, à 170 km de l'aéroport de Florence, à 230 km de celui de Rome. |
| PREISE | Zimmer ab 70 €, inklusive Frühstück. | PRIX | Chambre à partir de 70 €, petit-déjeuner inclus. |
| ZIMMER | 10 Zimmer (ohne Klimaanlage und Fernseher). | CHAMBRES | 10 chambres (non-climatisées, sans télévision). |
| KÜCHE | Das Gemüse stammt aus eigenem Anbau, das Olivenöl wird selbst gepresst. | RESTAURATION | Légumes du potager, l'huile d'olive est produite sur place. |
| GESCHICHTE | Das Grundstück gehörte einst der Florentiner Adelsfamilie del Grillo, die hier im 17. Jahrhundert einen Palast baute. Aus seiner Ruine entstand 1995 die Locanda del Gallo. | HISTOIRE | Le terrain appartenait autrefois à la noble famille florentine del Grillo, qui y construisit un palais au XVIIe siècle. Du palais en ruine est née la Locanda del Gallo en 1995. |
| X-FAKTOR | Der Salzwasserpool im Garten. | LES « PLUS » | La piscine d'eau salée dans le jardin. |

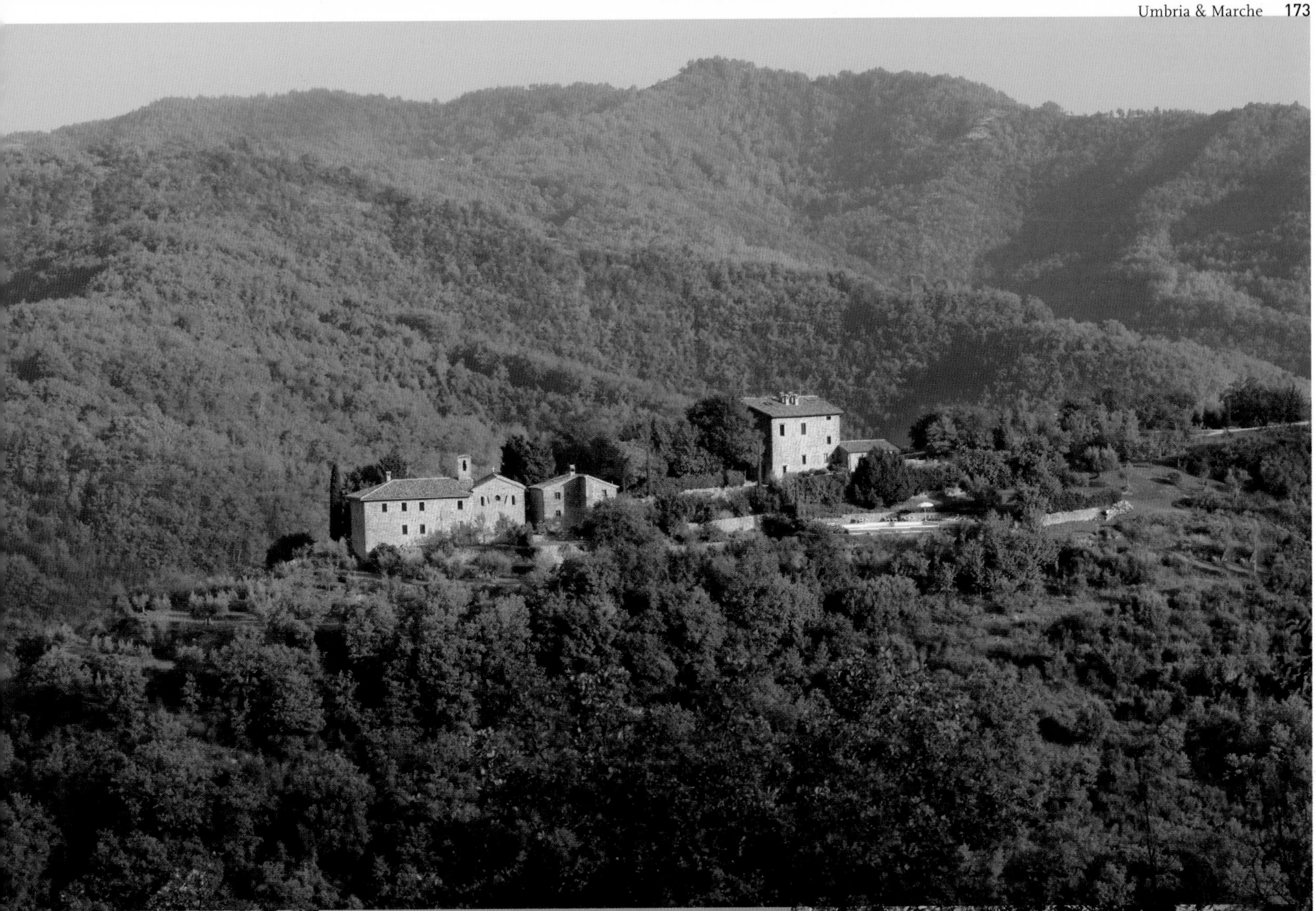

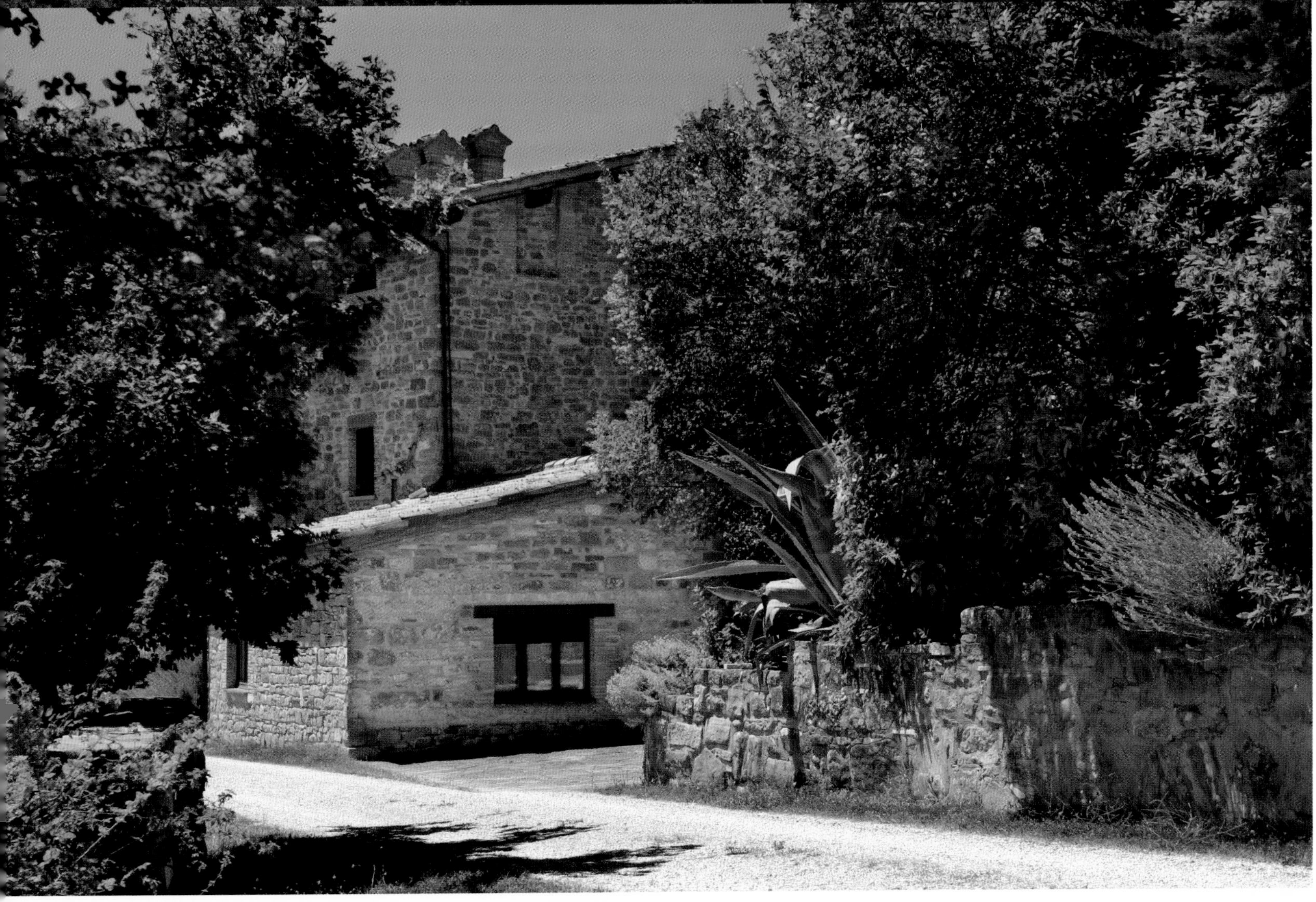

# In the Hills of the Marche
Casa San Ruffino, Montegiorgio

# Casa San Ruffino, Montegiorgio

**In the Hills of the Marche**

In one respect the Italians who live in the Marche are wholly un-Italian: they are not proponents of the "dolce far niente", the life of sweet idleness for which their compatriots are renowned. A lazy morning, an extended lunch break or a late dinner is not their way of doing things. They are hard-working and punctual, and were once regarded as the strictest tax-collectors for the papacy. In the rest of Italy they still hold on to the saying that it is better to have a corpse in your bed than a Marchigiano at the door. Perhaps the locals' passion for financial affairs was the reason why Ray and Claire Gorman made the Marche their home. The couple had been working for investment banks in England and were looking for a new challenge – which they found on a hilltop near Montegiorgio, where there was a wonderful view of the austere yet lovely landscape. Here the Gormans found an abandoned farm where the famous white Marchigiana cattle had been reared, and converted it into a simple bed & breakfast that is full of atmosphere. The four rooms with their low beams are fitted in dark wood and light-coloured fabrics, and all have en suite bathrooms. During the day guests at Casa San Ruffino can discover the Adriatic or the Apennines, the dripstone caves at Frasassi, the harbour of Ancona or the Renaissance architecture of Urbino. The pool and the open fireplace provide relaxation after a day out – because even when staying in the businesslike Marche, you have to practise a little bit of "dolce far niente".

**Book to pack: "The Worldwide Machine" by Paolo Volponi.**

| | |
|---|---|
| **Casa San Ruffino** | |
| Contrada Montese | |
| 63025 Montegiorgio | |
| Italy | |
| Tel./Fax +39 0734 962 753 | |
| info@casasanruffino.com | |
| www.casasanruffino.com | |
| **Open all year round** | |

| | |
|---|---|
| DIRECTIONS | In the Marche south of Ancona, 50 miles from the airport. |
| RATES | Rooms from 110 €, including breakfast. |
| ROOMS | 4 rooms. |
| FOOD | On request lunch and dinner are also served – delicious, down-to-earth Mediterranean dishes. |
| HISTORY | The farm dates from the 19th century, and Casa San Ruffino was opened in April 2007. |
| X-FACTOR | Warm-hearted hosts. |

## In den Hügeln der Marken

In einem Punkt sind die Italiener, die in den Marken leben, gänzlich unitalienisch: Sie sind keine Anhänger des »dolce far niente«, des süßen Nichtstuns, für das ihre Landsleute so berühmt sind. Ein vertrödelter Morgen, eine verlängerte Pause oder ein verspätetes Dinner passen nicht in ihr Konzept. Sie sind so fleißig wie pünktlich und galten einst als die strengsten Steuereintreiber des Papstes – noch heute kursiert im übrigen Italien der Spruch, es sei besser, einen Toten im Bett zu haben als einen Marchigiano vor der Tür. Vielleicht war diese Leidenschaft der Einheimischen für finanzielle Angelegenheiten der Grund dafür, dass Ray und Claire Gorman die Marken zu ihrer Wahlheimat machten. Das Ehepaar hatte in England bei Investment-Banken gearbeitet, suchte in Italien eine neue Herausforderung – und fand sie auf einem Hügel bei Montegiorgio, der eine traumhafte Sicht über die herb-süße Landschaft bot. Hier stand ein verlassener Bauernhof, auf dem die berühmten weißen Marchigiana-Rinder gezüchtet worden waren und den die Gormans in ein schlichtes, sehr atmosphärisches Bed & Breakfast verwandelten. Die vier Zimmer unter alten Deckenbalken sind mit dunklem Holz sowie hellen Stoffen eingerichtet und besitzen alle eigene Bäder. Tagsüber erkunden die Gäste der Casa San Ruffino die Adria oder die Apenninen, die Tropfsteinhöhlen von Frasassi, den Hafen von Ancona oder die Renaissance-Bauten von Urbino. Entspannung nach den Exkursionen bieten Pool und Kamin – denn selbst wenn man sich in den geschäftigen Marken befindet: Ein bisschen »dolce far niente« muss sein.
**Buchtipp: »Die Weltmaschine« von Paolo Volponi.**

## Dans les collines des Marches

Il y a un point sur lequel les habitants des Marches se différencient des autres Italiens : ils ne sont pas fervents du « dolce farniente », cette douce oisiveté qui fait la célébrité de leurs compatriotes. Une matinée passée à musarder, une pause un peu trop longue ou un dîner en retard les contrarient. Aussi travailleurs que ponctuels, ils étaient autrefois considérés comme les plus sévères collecteurs d'impôts du pape – aujourd'hui encore, on entend dire dans les autres régions d'Italie qu'il vaut mieux avoir un mort dans son lit qu'un Marchigiano à sa porte. Mais cette passion des habitants de la région pour la finance est peut-être la raison pour laquelle Ray et Claire Gorman ont choisi de s'installer dans les Marches. Après avoir travaillé en Angleterre dans des banques d'investissement, ils ont voulu relever de nouveaux défis en Italie. Ils ont trouvé ce qu'ils cherchaient près de Montegiorgio, sur une colline qui offre une vue sublime sur le paysage rude et doux à la fois, transformant une ferme abandonnée – on y pratiquait l'élevage des célèbres bœufs de la race Marchiagiana –, en une sobre maison d'hôtes pleine d'atmosphère. Les quatre chambres dotées de vieux plafonds à poutres sont meublées et décorées de bois sombre et d'étoffes claires et possèdent une salle de bains attenante. Pendant la journée, les hôtes de la Casa San Ruffino explorent la mer Adriatique ou les Apennins, les grottes de Frasassi, le port d'Ancône ou les constructions Renaissance d'Urbin. Après les excursions, la piscine et un bon feu dans la cheminée invitent à la détente : un peu de farniente, même ici dans les Marches.
**Livre à emporter : « Le Système d'Anteo Crocioni » de Paolo Volponi.**

| ANREISE | In den Marken südlich von Ancona gelegen, 80 km vom Flughafen entfernt. |
|---|---|
| PREISE | Zimmer ab 110 €, inklusive Frühstück. |
| ZIMMER | 4 Zimmer. |
| KÜCHE | Auf Wunsch wird auch Mittag- und Abendessen serviert – die mediterranen Gerichte sind bodenständig und köstlich. |
| GESCHICHTE | Der Bauernhof stammt aus dem 19. Jahrhundert. Die Casa San Ruffino wurde im April 2007 eröffnet. |
| X-FAKTOR | Die herzlichen Gastgeber. |

| ACCÈS | Dans les Marches, au sud d'Ancône, à 80 km de l'aéroport. |
|---|---|
| PRIX | Chambre à partir de 110 €, petit-déjeuner inclus. |
| CHAMBRES | 4 chambres. |
| RESTAURATION | Le déjeuner et le dîner sont servis à la demande – les menus méditerranéens sont simples et délicieux. |
| HISTOIRE | La ferme date du XIXᵉ siècle. La Casa San Ruffino a ouvert ses portes en avril 2007. |
| LES « PLUS » | La gentillesse des hôtes. |

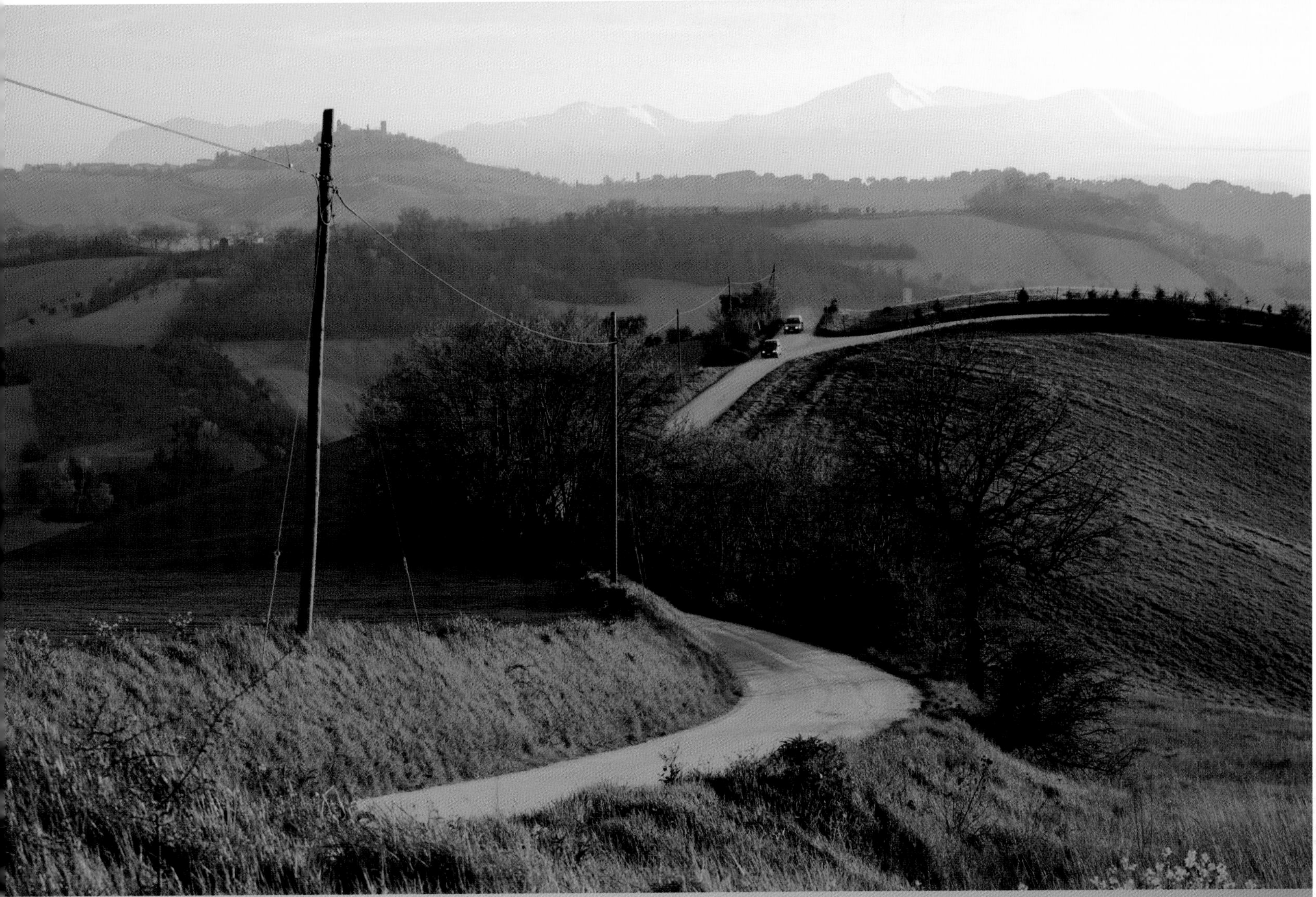

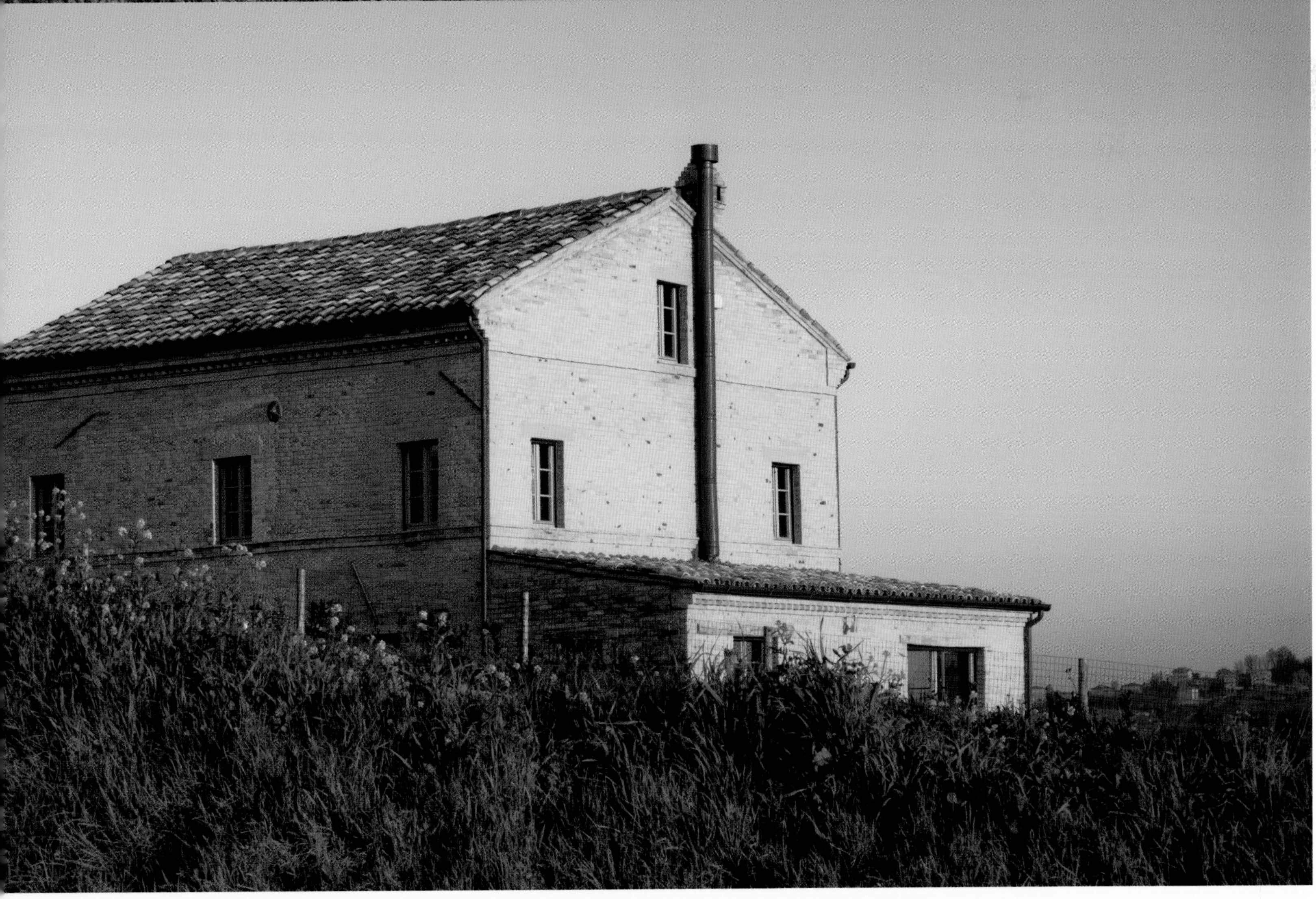

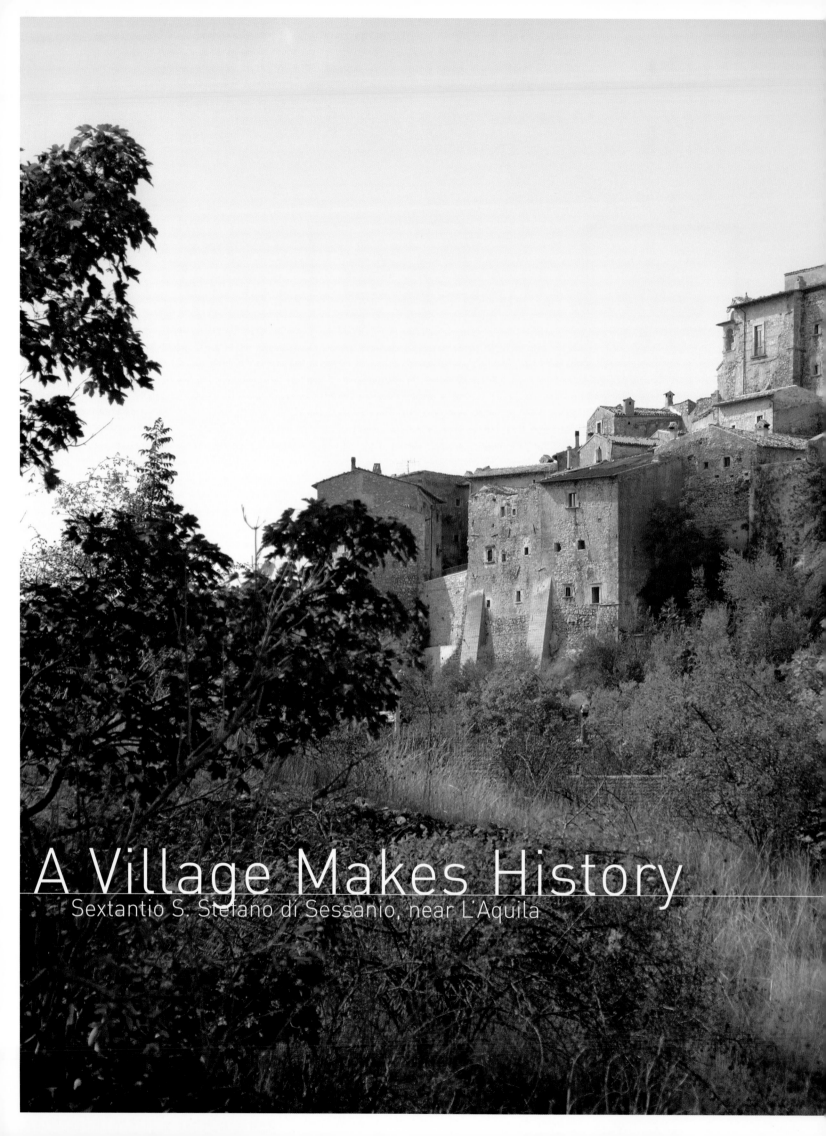

# A Village Makes History
Sextantio S. Stefano di Sessanio, near L'Aquila

# Sextantio S. Stefano di Sessanio, near L'Aquila

**Open all year round**

### A Village Makes History

Daniele Kihlgren discovered the village purely by chance: the son of an industrialist from Milan, he got lost on his motorbike in the Abruzzi mountains and made a stop near Santo Stefano di Sessanio – a break that was to lead to the project of a lifetime. He was so fascinated by this medieval shepherds' settlement, although it had fallen into ruin and was almost deserted, that he revived it, investing his inheritance in the village, buying part of it and transforming it into one of Italy's most unusual hotels. His "albergo diffuso" (scattered hotel) comprises 27 rooms in several different houses, which were restored authentically in the archaic Arte Povera style with the advice of archaeologists, archivists and locals. From the soot-blackened walls to the wooden beds with sheep's-wool mattresses and the heavy roof beams, everything is original or true to the original. If the interiors were not equipped with underfloor heating, electric lighting and bathrooms by Philippe Starck, guests would think they were living in the depths of the Middle Ages. In order to present as genuine a picture as possible of the culture of the Abruzzi, Kihlgren undertook research into old regional recipes, fitted out ateliers where the work was done using historic methods and founded his own music ensemble. His energy even extends beyond the boundaries of the village: on his motorbike he now roams throughout southern Italy in search of further villages where the Sextantio group that he founded can continue to use the past to create a future.
**Book to pack: "The Last World" by Christoph Ransmayr.**

**Sextantio S. Stefano di Sessanio**
c/o Sextantio srl
Via Principe Umberto
67020 Santo Stefano di Sessanio
Italy
Tel./Fax +39 0862 899 112
info@sextantio.it and reservation@sextantio.it
www.sextantio.it
**Open all year round**

| | |
|---|---|
| DIRECTIONS | At an altitude of 4,101 feet; 16 miles from L'Aquila, 108 miles from Rome Airport. |
| RATES | Rooms from 220 €, including breakfast. |
| ROOMS | 27 rooms in 7 houses. |
| FOOD | The restaurant serves rustic food using typical medieval ingredients such as lentils and chickpeas; there is a wine bar and a tearoom. |
| HISTORY | The village once belonged to the Medici estates and produced sheep's wool; the hotel opened in September 2005. |
| X-FACTOR | A ban on new construction means that the village will remain unspoiled. |

## Ein Dorf schreibt Geschichte

Daniele Kihlgren entdeckte das Dorf ganz zufällig: Der Industriellensohn aus Mailand hatte sich mit seinem Motorrad in den Bergen der Abruzzen verfahren, legte in der Nähe von Santo Stefano di Sessanio einen Stopp ein – und aus der kurzen Pause wurde das Projekt seines Lebens. Er war von der mittelalterlichen Hirtensiedlung, obgleich sie zur Ruine verfallen und fast verlassen war, so fasziniert, dass er sie wiederbelebte – er investierte sein Erbe in den Ort, kaufte einen Teil davon und verwandelte ihn in eine der ungewöhnlichsten Herbergen Italiens. Sein »albergo diffuso« (verstreutes Hotel) umfasst 27 Zimmer in mehreren Häusern, die authentisch und unter Beratung von Archäologen, Archivaren sowie Einheimischen im archaischen Stil der Arte Povera renoviert wurden. Von den rußgeschwärzten Mauern über die Holzbetten mit Schafswollmatratzen bis hin zu den schweren Deckenbalken ist alles original oder originalgetreu – wäre das Interieur nicht mit Fußbodenheizung, elektrischem Licht und Philippe-Starck-Bädern ausgestattet, man könnte meinen, im tiefsten Mittelalter zu Gast zu sein. Um so unverfälscht wie möglich von der Kultur der Abruzzen zu erzählen, ließ Kihlgren auch nach alten Rezepten der Region forschen, richtete Werkstätten ein, in denen mit historischen Techniken gearbeitet wird, und gründete ein eigenes Musikensemble. Seine Energie reicht sogar über die Dorfgrenzen hinaus: Er rollt auf seinem Motorrad inzwischen durch ganz Süditalien und sucht nach weiteren Orten, denen die von ihm gegründete Sextantio-Gruppe mithilfe der Vergangenheit eine Zukunft geben kann.

**Buchtipp: »Die letzte Welt« von Christoph Ransmayr.**

## Retour aux sources

Daniele Kihlgren a découvert le village tout à fait par hasard : ce fils d'industriels de Milan s'était perdu en faisant une virée en moto dans les Abruzzes ; il s'arrêta à proximité de Santo Stefano di Sessanio, et de cette petite pause naquit le projet de sa vie. Le petit bourg médiéval n'était plus que ruines et pratiquement abandonné, mais il le fascina tellement qu'il lui rendit la vie – il investit son héritage dans le village, en acheta une partie et le transforma en l'une des auberges les plus insolites d'Italie. Son « albergo diffuso » (auberge éparpillée) comprend 27 chambres réparties dans plusieurs maisons, restaurées de manière authentique dans le style archaïque de l'Arte Povera grâce aux conseils des archéologues, des archivistes et des gens du pays. Des murs noircis de suie aux lourdes poutres de plafond en passant par les lits en bois garnis de matelas pure laine, tout est original ou fidèlement reproduit. Et on pourrait se croire au plus profond du Moyen Age, si ces intérieurs ne disposaient pas de chauffage au sol, de lumière électrique et de salles de bains Philippe Starck. Pour transmettre le plus authentiquement possible la culture des Abruzzes, Kihlgren a aussi fait rechercher des vieilles recettes régionales, il a créé des ateliers travaillant avec des techniques historiques et fondé un ensemble musical. Mais il lui reste beaucoup d'énergie : sillonnant l'Italie du Sud sur sa moto, il est à la recherche d'autres lieux à qui le groupe Sextantio, qu'il a fondé, peut donner un avenir grâce à l'histoire.

**Livre à emporter : « Le Dernier des mondes » de Christoph Ransmayr.**

| | | | |
|---|---|---|---|
| ANREISE | Auf 1.250 m Höhe gelegen; 27 km von L'Aquila, 175 km vom Flughafen Rom entfernt. | ACCÈS | Situé à 1250 m d'altitude à 27 km de L'Aquila et 175 km de l'aéroport de Rome. |
| PREISE | Zimmer ab 220 €, inklusive Frühstück. | PRIX | Chambre à partir de 220 €, petit-déjeuner inclus. |
| ZIMMER | 27 Zimmer in 7 Häusern. | CHAMBRES | 27 chambres dans 7 maisons. |
| KÜCHE | Das Restaurant serviert Rustikales mit typisch mittelalterlichen Zutaten wie Linsen oder Kichererbsen. Es gibt eine Weinbar und einen Teeraum. | RESTAURATION | Le restaurant sert des plats rustiques à base d'ingrédients typiques du Moyen Age, tels les pois chiches et les lentilles. Il y a un bar à vin et une « tisaneria ». |
| GESCHICHTE | Einst gehörte das Dorf zu den Ländereien der Medici und produzierte Schafswolle. Das Hotel eröffnete im September 2005. | HISTOIRE | Le village était situé sur les terres des Médicis et produisait de la laine. L'hôtel a ouvert ses portes en septembre 2005. |
| X-FAKTOR | Dank eines Neubauverbots wird der Ort ursprünglich bleiben. | LES « PLUS » | Les nouvelles constructions étant interdites, le site conservera son caractère authentique. |

# A Beacon of Style

Faro Capo Spartivento, Capo Spartivento

# Faro Capo Spartivento,
# Capo Spartivento

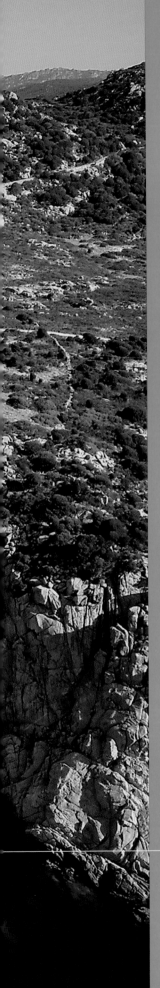

## A Beacon of Style

Travellers with a taste for adventure but also for the avant-garde and aesthetics should put Faro Capo Spartivento right at the top of their list of places to be visited. High above the southernmost point of Sardinia, the lighthouse is the only building on the "cape that divides the wind". It looks down on a landscape with an eventful history of Saracen raids and naval battles, and breathtaking natural beauty: the cobalt-blue sea and the jagged rocks look so primeval and untouched that it is hard to believe that this is the jet set's favourite Italian island in the third millennium. King Vittorio Emanuele had the lighthouse built in 1856, and to this day a historic ornament with the royal initials crowns the entrance, and the king would surely have appreciated the new interior designed by the owner, Alessio Raggio. He combines modern white sofas with vintage furniture from all over the world – highly eclectic and inventive, as shown by the Turkish carts that were made into beds and the Mongolian quern that supports a washbasin. The ambience, too, is exclusive: a maximum of twelve guests can stay here at one time to be pampered by staff who are almost invisible, like friendly spirits. The two apartments next to the main house are especially private and have a heavenly extra touch. The glass ceiling above the bed allows a view of the stars and the beam from the lighthouse: Faro Capo Spartivento is still in operation.

**Book to pack:** "Reeds in the Wind" by Grazia Deledda.

| | |
|---|---|
| **Faro Capo Spartivento** | |
| Commune di Domus de Maria | |
| 09010 Chia | |
| Italy | |
| Tel. +39 3333 129 638 | |
| info@farocapospartivento.com | |
| www.farocapospartivento.com | |
| **Open all year round** | |

| | |
|---|---|
| DIRECTIONS | 31 miles from Cagliari Airport. |
| RATES | Suite from 1,800 € per week, exclusive rental of the whole lighthouse from 10,000 € per week. All prices include cook and butler. |
| ROOMS | 4 suites and 2 apartments. |
| FOOD | The private cook prepares Mediterranean menus according to guests' wishes. The wines to match are stored in the cellar, an old cistern. |
| HISTORY | The lighthouse was converted between 2006 and 2009 and equipped with state-of-the-art technology such as solar and recycling systems. |
| X-FACTOR | The wood terrace with a telescope and infinity pool. |

## Mit Signalwirkung

Wer einen Sinn fürs Abenteuer hat und zugleich für Avant-
garde und Ästhetik, der sollte den Faro Capo Spartivento
weit oben auf seine Wunschliste künftiger Reiseziele setzen.
Hoch über dem südlichsten Punkt Sardiniens gelegen, ist
der Leuchtturm das einzige Gebäude auf dem »Kap, das
den Wind teilt« und blickt über eine Landschaft mit einer
spannenden Geschichte voller Sarazenen-Angriffe und
Seeschlachten sowie einer atemberaubenden Natur: Das
kobaltblaue Meer und die zerklüfteten Felsen wirken so
ursprünglich und unberührt, dass man kaum glauben kann,
im dritten Jahrtausend und auf der italienischen Lieblings-
insel des Jetsets zu sein. Errichtet wurde der Leuchtturm
1856 im Auftrag Vittorio Emanueles – noch heute krönt ein
antikes Ornament mit den Initialen des Königs den Eingang,
und der Regent hätte sicherlich auch am neuen Interieur
Gefallen gefunden, das Besitzer Alessio Raggio gestaltet hat.
Er mischt moderne weiße Sofas mit Vintage-Mobiliar aus
aller Welt – sehr eklektisch und erfinderisch, wie die türkischen Karren beweisen, aus denen Tagesbetten wurden,
oder der Mörser aus der Mongolei, der ein Waschbecken
stützt. Exklusiv ist das Ambiente ebenfalls: Maximal zwölf
Gäste können hier zur gleichen Zeit wohnen und werden
von fast unsichtbaren guten Geistern verwöhnt. Die beiden
Apartments neben dem Haupthaus bieten besonders viel
Privatsphäre und ein himmlisches Extra noch dazu: Durch
die Glasdecke über dem Bett sieht man die Sterne und kann
den Lichtkegel des Leuchtturms verfolgen – denn der Faro
Capo Spartivento ist noch immer in Betrieb.

**Buchtipp: »Schilf im Wind« von Grazia Deledda.**

## Un signal lumineux

Ceux qui aiment l'aventure, mais prisent aussi l'avant-garde
et l'esthétique, devraient inscrire Faro Capo Spartivento tout
en haut de la liste de leurs futurs voyages. Ce phare qui surplombe l'extrémité sud de la Sardaigne, le seul édifice sur le
« cap qui divise le vent », pose ses regards sur un paysage
d'une beauté à couper le souffle, dont le passé captivant est
rempli d'attaques sarrasines et de batailles navales. La mer
bleu cobalt et les falaises déchiquetées ont l'air si primitives
et si sauvages que l'on a peine à croire que l'on se trouve, au
XXIe siècle, sur l'île italienne préférée de la jet-set. Le phare
a été construit en 1856 sur l'ordre de Victor-Emmanuel II de
Savoie – ses initiales sont gravées sur un ornement ancien
au-dessus de l'entrée –, qui aurait sans doute apprécié les
nouveaux aménagements du propriétaire, Alessio Raggio.
Celui-ci marie des canapés blancs modernes à des meubles
vintage venus de partout, de manière très éclectique et
créative ainsi qu'en témoignent les charrettes turques trans-
formées en lit ou le mortier mongol qui soutient un lavabo.
L'ambiance est elle aussi exclusive : 12 hôtes maximum
peuvent loger ici en même temps et sont chouchoutés par
un personnel presque invisible. Les deux appartements situés
à côté de la maison principale offrent beaucoup d'intimité
et un extra « céleste » en prime : le plafond en verre au-
dessus du lit permet de voir les étoiles et de suivre le cône
de lumière du phare – car le Faro Capo Spartivento est
toujours en activité.

**Livre à emporter : « Des Roseaux sous le vent » de Grazia
Deledda.**

| | |
|---|---|
| ANREISE | 50 km vom Flughafen Cagliari entfernt. |
| PREISE | Suite ab 1.800 € pro Woche, Exklusivmiete des ganzen Leuchtturms ab 10.000 € pro Woche. Alle Preise inklusive Koch und Butler. |
| ZIMMER | 4 Suiten und 2 Apartments. |
| KÜCHE | Der Privatkoch bereitet mediterrane Menüs nach Wunsch zu. Die passenden Weine lagern im Keller, einer alten Zisterne. |
| GESCHICHTE | Der Leuchtturm wurde 2006–2009 umgebaut und mit modernster Technik sowie Solar- und Recyclingsystemen ausgestattet. |
| X-FAKTOR | Die Holzterrasse mit Teleskop und Infinity-Pool. |

| | |
|---|---|
| ACCÈS | À 50 km de l'aéroport de Cagliari. |
| PRIX | Suite à partir de 1800 € par semaine, location du phare à partir de 10 000 € par semaine. Cuisinier et maître d'hôtel inclus. |
| CHAMBRES | 4 suites et 2 appartements. |
| RESTAURATION | Le cuisinier prépare des plats méditerranéens selon les désirs des hôtes. Les vins sont entreposés dans une citerne reconvertie en cave. |
| HISTOIRE | Le phare a été transformé en 2006–2009 et équipé des techniques les plus modernes, tels les capteurs solaires ou le système de recyclage. |
| LES « PLUS » | Terrasse avec télescope et piscine à débordement. |

# Above the Healing Waters
Mezzatorre, Ischia

# Mezzatorre, Ischia

Open from the middle
of April to the end of October

**Above the Healing Waters**

Thermal waters are not just thermal waters here – bubbling up from the depths of the earth, pleasantly warm and with a wealth of minerals sufficient to ease every imaginable complaint, from asthma to rheumatism. No, the thermal water on Ischia comes from the tears of a giant: according to a myth, in primeval times the giant Typhon plunged into the sea after a dispute with Zeus and was buried beneath rocks by the wrathful father of the gods. Ischia was formed by the rocks, and below the island the giant raged and cried for so long that Aphrodite took pity on him and transformed his tears into healing springs. These legendary waters became Ischia's main source of income in the course of time. Today almost every hotel has its own thermal bath, where guests can take time out with hydrotherapy and fango treatments. Mezzatorre Resort & Spa, which lies on the north-west coast and was built around a 16th-century watchtower, is a particularly stylish spa. The restored torre houses truly superb suites – with a view so breathtaking that they seem to be suspended between heaven and earth. There is also a wonderful view, though closer to the ground, from the pool at the edge of a cliff and the two restaurants, which are among the best gourmet destinations on Ischia. The spa itself makes do without a panorama – but its treatments with giant's tears are best enjoyed with eyes closed anyway.
**Book to pack: "The Dogs Bark" by Truman Capote.**

| | |
|---|---|
| **Mezzatorre Resort & Spa** | |
| Via Mezzatorre 23 | |
| 80075 Forio d'Ischia | |
| Italy | |
| Tel. +39 081 986 111 | |
| Fax +39 081 986 015 | |
| info@mezzatorre.it | |
| www.mezzatorre.it | |

| | |
|---|---|
| DIRECTIONS | In the bay of San Montano, 5 miles from the harbour (45 min by fast boat to Naples). |
| RATES | Rooms from 210 €, suites from 520 €, including breakfast. |
| ROOMS | 45 rooms and 12 suites. |
| FOOD | In "Chandelier" Mediterranean meals are served by candlelight, while traditional Neapolitan dishes are prepared in "Sciuè Sciuè" by the pool. |
| HISTORY | The resort was designed by the Izzo architectural studio in Naples and opened in 1989. |
| X-FACTOR | A walk at sundown in the park, where exotic plants thrive. |

## Hoch über dem heilenden Wasser

Thermalwasser ist hier nicht bloß Thermalwasser, tief aus der Erde sprudelnd, wohltuend warm und angereichert mit genug Mineralstoffen, um vom Asthma bis zum Rheuma alle erdenklichen Leiden zu lindern. Nein, auf Ischia besteht das Thermalwasser aus den Tränen eines Riesen: Die Sage erzählt, dass vor Urzeiten der Gigant Tyhon nach einem Streit mit Zeus ins Meer stürzte und vom zürnenden Göttervater unter Felsen begraben wurde. Aus den Steinen entstand Ischia, und unter der Insel tobte und heulte der Riese so lange, bis Aphrodite Mitleid mit ihm hatte und seine Tränen in Heil bringende Quellen verwandelte. Die legendären Wasser sind im Lauf der Zeit zu Ischias wichtigsten Einnahmequellen geworden – heute besitzt so gut wie jedes Hotel eine eigene Therme, in der man bei Hydrotherapien und Fango-Packungen eine Auszeit vom Alltag nehmen kann. Besonders stilvoll geht dies im Mezzatorre Resort & Spa, das an der Nordwestküste liegt und rund um einen Wachturm aus dem 16. Jahrhundert erbaut wurde. Der restaurierte Torre beherbergt die herrlichsten Suiten – mit einer so atemberaubenden Sicht, dass man glaubt, zwischen Himmel und Meer zu schweben. Einen traumhaften Blick, wenn auch mit etwas mehr Bodenhaftung, eröffnen auch der am Rand eines Kliffs gelegene Pool und die beiden Restaurants, die zu Ischias besten Gourmetadressen gehören. Das Spa selbst verzichtet auf eine Panoramaposition – doch die Anwendungen mit den Tränen des Riesen genießt man ohnehin am besten mit geschlossenen Augen.

**Buchtipp: »Die Hunde bellen« von Truman Capote.**

## Au-dessus des eaux bienfaisantes

Ici, l'eau thermale n'est pas seulement une eau jaillissant des profondeurs, agréablement chaude et enrichie de suffisamment de minéraux pour adoucir tous les maux, de l'asthme aux rhumatismes – non, à Ischia l'eau thermale est née des larmes d'un géant : la légende rapporte qu'il y a bien longtemps le géant Typhon qui avait osé défier Zeus, fut précipité par celui-ci dans la mer et enterré sous des rochers. De ces rochers naquit Ischia et le géant furieux hurla si longtemps sous terre que Aphrodite eut pitié de lui et transforma ses larmes en source aux vertus thérapeutiques. Au fil du temps, les eaux mythiques sont devenues la principale source de revenus d'Ischia : aujourd'hui, chaque hôtel ou presque possède ses thermes proposant balnéothérapie et bains de boue aux vertus relaxantes. On peut ainsi oublier le quotidien de la manière la plus élégante au Mezzatorre Resort & Spa, qui se trouve au nord-ouest de l'île et a été aménagé autour d'une tour de garde du XVI$^e$ siècle. La tour restaurée abrite des suites de toute beauté, offrant une vue si prodigieuse que l'on croit planer entre ciel et terre. La piscine située au bord d'une falaise et les deux restaurants qui font partie des meilleures adresses d'Ischia proposent aussi un panorama superbe, quoique moins aérien. Rien de tout cela au spa mais, de toute façon, c'est les yeux fermés qu'il faut apprécier les « larmes du géant ».

**Livre à emporter : « Les Chiens aboient » de Truman Capote.**

| | |
|---|---|
| ANREISE | In der Bucht von San Montano gelegen, 8 km vom Hafen entfernt (45 min mit dem Schnellboot bis Neapel). |
| PREISE | Zimmer ab 210 €, Suite ab 520 €, inklusive Frühstück. |
| ZIMMER | 45 Zimmer und 12 Suiten. |
| KÜCHE | Das »Chandelier« serviert mediterrane Menüs im Kerzenschein, das »Sciuè Sciuè« am Pool traditionelle neapolitanische Gerichte. |
| GESCHICHTE | Das Resort wurde vom Architekturstudio Izzo in Neapel gestaltet und 1989 eröffnet. |
| X-FAKTOR | Ein Spaziergang bei Sonnenuntergang im Park, in dem exotische Pflanzen gedeihen. |

| | |
|---|---|
| ACCÈS | Dans la baie de San Montano, à 8 km du port (à 45 min de Naples en bateau à moteur). |
| PRIX | Chambre à partir de 210 €, suite à partir de 520 €, petit-déjeuner inclus. |
| CHAMBRES | 45 chambres et 12 suites. |
| RESTAURATION | Le « Chandelier » offre des menus méditerranéens à la lueur des bougies, le « Sciuè Sciuè », au bord de la piscine, des plats traditionnels napolitains. |
| HISTOIRE | Conçu par le cabinet d'architectes Izzo à Naples, l'hôtel a ouvert ses portes en 1989. |
| LES « PLUS » | Une promenade au soleil couchant dans le parc où poussent des plantes exotiques. |

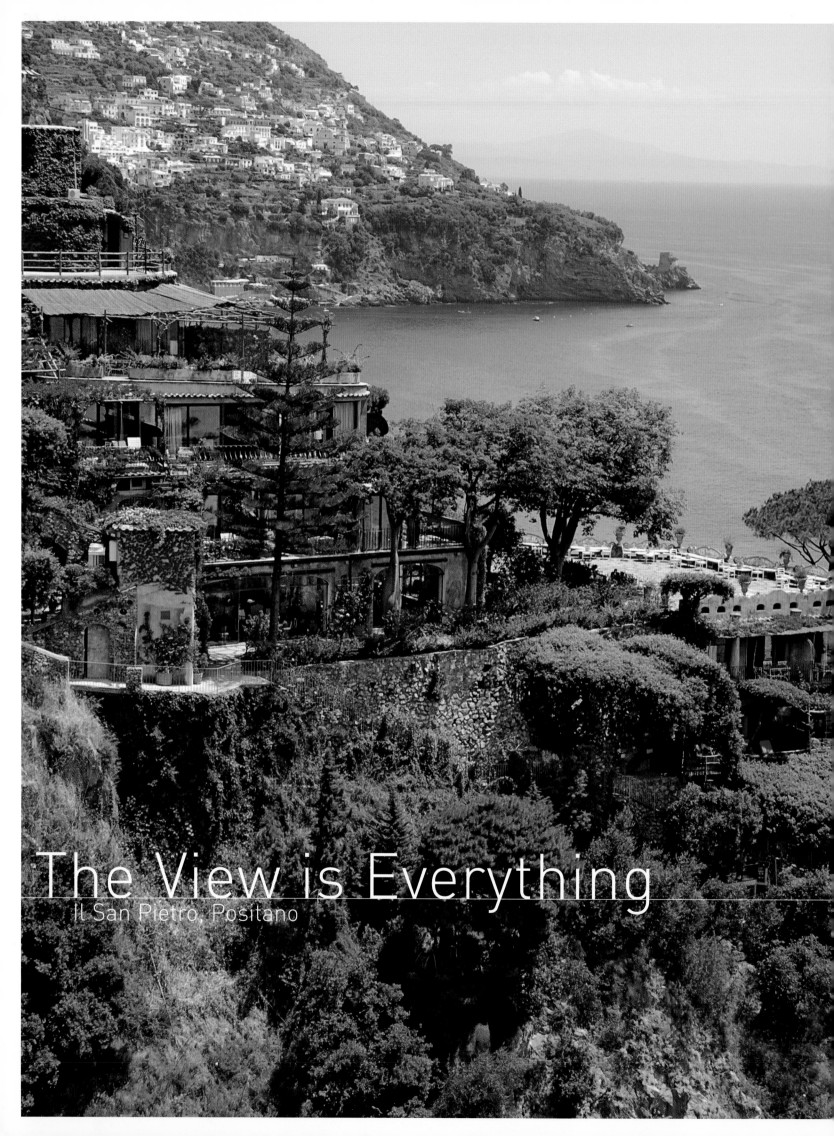

# The View is Everything
Il San Pietro, Positano

# Il San Pietro, Positano

**The View is Everything**

His trademark was a wide-brimmed straw hat. He was so stylish that he still looked irresistible in shorts and sandals, and even Hollywood stars described his parties as legendary: Carlo Cinque, a self-made man and visionary who gave Positano its finest hotel and most spectacular look-out point: the Il San Pietro. He had the hotel built in the 1960s on terraces on a rock projecting far into the sea on the Amalfi coast, and took advice for the work solely from an electrical engineer – he himself carried out the tasks of architect, construction engineer, site supervisor and interior designer. And decades before the profession of "guest relations manager" was invented, Carlo Cinque was a master of the art of caring for his hotel guests. Today his niece Virginia and her sons display the same talent in running Il San Pietro, and they are bringing off the feat of discreetly updating the estate without destroying its stylish ambience. They decorated the panorama terrace with ceramic tiles that depict marine scenes in 17th-century style, established an excellent spa beneath lemon trees and were so successful at refining traditional cooking that they were awarded a Michelin star. Right next to their private beach they opened a second restaurant and named it "Carlino" in honour of their great role model. To travel the 288 feet in height between the reception and the restaurant, guests take a lift. The lift shaft was once hewn straight from the rock – by Carlo Cinque personally, of course.

**Book to pack:** "Lady Windermere's Fan" by Oscar Wilde – filmed on the Amalfi coast with the title "A Good Woman".

**Il San Pietro di Positano**
Via Laurito 2
84017 Positano
Italy
Tel. +39 089 875 455
Fax +39 089 811 449
reservations@ilsanpietro.it
www.ilsanpietro.it
**Open from the beginning**
**of April to the end of October**

| | |
|---|---|
| DIRECTIONS | 37 miles south of Naples. |
| RATES | Rooms from 420 €, including breakfast. |
| ROOMS | 61 rooms, all with their own terrace and a sea view. |
| FOOD | The candlelight dinners in "Il San Pietro" are extremely romantic. The informal "Carlino" serves salads from the hotel's own garden. |
| HISTORY | Il San Pietro opened on 29 June 1970, on the feast day of St Peter. It is a member of Relais & Châteaux. |
| X-FACTOR | In summer a boat trip along the Amalfi coast is organised free of charge every morning. |

## Alles ist Aussicht

Ein Strohhut mit breiter Krempe war sein Markenzeichen. Er hatte so viel Stil, dass er sogar in Shorts und Sandalen umwerfend aussah, und seine Partys bezeichneten selbst Stars aus Hollywood als legendär: Carlo Cinque, der Selfmademan und Visionär, der Positano mit Il San Pietro sein schönstes Hotel und seinen spektakulärsten Aussichtspunkt gab. Terrassenartig ließ er das Haus in den 1960ern an einen weit vorspringenden Felsen der Amalfiküste bauen und holte sich dabei lediglich den Rat eines Elektroingenieurs – als Architekt, Statiker, Bauleiter und Ausstatter fungierte er höchstpersönlich. Ebenso als Gästebetreuer in seinem Hotel – Jahrzehnte, ehe man den Beruf des »Guest Relation Manager« erfand, war Carlo Cinque bereits Meister dieses Fachs. Heute führen seine Nichte Virginia und ihre Söhne Il San Pietro mit demselben Talent und bringen das Kunststück fertig, das Anwesen dezent aufzufrischen, ohne sein stilvolles Ambiente zu zerstören. Sie ließen die Panoramaterrasse mit Keramikfliesen schmücken, die maritime Szenen im Stil des 17. Jahrhunderts zeigen, richteten unter Zitronenbäumen ein exzellentes Spa ein und verfeinerten die traditionelle Küche so gelungen, dass sie einen Michelin-Stern erhielt. Direkt am Privatstrand eröffneten sie ein zweites Lokal und benannten es zu Ehren ihres großen Vorbilds »Carlino«. Die 88 Meter Höhenunterschied zwischen Rezeption und Restaurant überwindet man im Lift, dessen Schacht einst direkt in den Fels geschlagen wurde – natürlich von Carlo Cinque persönlich.

**Buchtipp: »Lady Windermeres Fächer« von Oscar Wilde – wurde an der Amalfiküste verfilmt (»Good Woman – Ein Sommer in Amalfi«).**

## La mer et le ciel

Carlo Cinque ne quittait jamais son chapeau de paille à large bord ; même en shorts et nu-pieds, il avait une allure folle ; quant à ses fêtes, les stars hollywoodiennes les trouvaient légendaires. Le self-made-man visionnaire qui a donné à Positano son plus bel hôtel et son point de vue le plus spectaculaire fit bâtir la maison en terrasse sur un promontoire de la côte amalfitaine au cours des années 1960. Il n'écouta que les conseils d'un électro-ingénieur, faisant lui-même office d'architecte, d'ingénieur, de chef de chantier et de décorateur. Il continua sur sa lancée avec ses hôtes – des décennies avant que l'on ait inventé le métier de « guest relation manager », Carlo Cinque était déjà passé maître dans cet art. Aujourd'hui, sa nièce Virginia et ses fils dirigent le Il San Pietro avec la même virtuosité et ont réussi à moderniser discrètement les lieux sans détruire leur ambiance élégante. La terrasse panoramique a été pavée de carreaux de céramique montrant des scènes maritimes dans le style du XVIIe siècle, un spa a été aménagé sous les citronniers et la cuisine traditionnelle perfectionnée de telle manière que le restaurant a obtenu une étoile au Michelin. Les propriétaires ont ouvert un second établissement sur la plage privée et l'ont baptisé « Carlino » en hommage à leur modèle. Un ascenseur relie la réception au restaurant situé 88 mètres plus haut. Il a été directement creusé dans le rocher – par Carlo Cinque, évidemment.

**Livre à emporter : « L'Eventail de Lady Windermere » d'Oscar Wilde (son adaptation cinématographique « La Séductrice » a été tournée sur la côte d'Amalfi).**

| ANREISE | 60 km südlich von Neapel gelegen. |
|---|---|
| PREISE | Zimmer ab 420 €, inklusive Frühstück. |
| ZIMMER | 61 Zimmer, alle mit eigener Terrasse und Meerblick. |
| KÜCHE | Die Candlelight-Dinner im »Il San Pietro« sind sehr romantisch. Das legere »Carlino« serviert Salate aus dem hoteleigenen Garten. |
| GESCHICHTE | Il San Pietro eröffnete am 29. Juni 1970, dem Namenstag des Heiligen Peter. Es ist Mitglied bei Relais & Châteaux. |
| X-FAKTOR | Im Sommer wird jeden Morgen ein kostenloser Bootsausflug entlang der Amalfiküste angeboten. |

| ACCÈS | A 60 km au sud de Naples. |
|---|---|
| PRIX | Chambre à partir de 420 €, petit-déjeuner inclus. |
| CHAMBRES | 61 chambres, toutes dotées d'une terrasse avec vue sur la mer. |
| RESTAURATION | Dîner aux chandelles très romantique au « Il San Pietro ». Le « Carlino » sert des salades provenant des jardins de l'hôtel. |
| HISTOIRE | Il San Pietro a ouvert ses portes le 29 juin 1970, jour de la Saint-Pierre. Il est membre des Relais & Châteaux. |
| LES « PLUS » | L'été, une excursion gratuite en bateau le long de la côte amalfitaine est proposée. |

# With a Panoramic View
Hotel Palumbo, Ravello

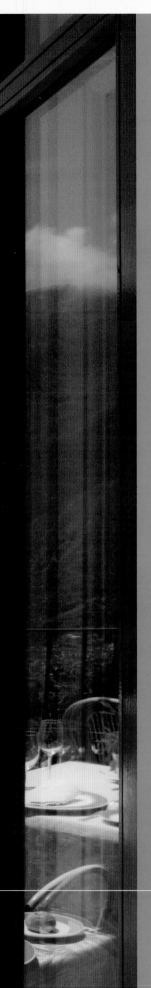

# Hotel Palumbo, Ravello

**With a Panoramic View**

It is the breathtaking view, the perfect panorama, that makes Ravello such a special place. This little town, at an elevation of 1,000 feet above the Amalfi coast, has a sweeping view of mountains and the sea – framed by sculptures in stone with a patina, purple-glowing bougainvillea or the boughs of a pine tree. Boccaccio sang the praises of Ravello in "The Decameron", and later D. H. Lawrence wrote "Lady Chatterley's Lover" and André Gide "The Immoralist" here. In Ravello, Richard Wagner found Klingsor's magic garden and Edvard Grieg inspiration for "Peer Gynt". Many of these famous visitors were guests at the Hotel Palumbo, which has been one of the finest places to stay in Ravello for over 130 years. The heart of the house is the historic Palazzo Confalone, where the rooms are opulently and classically furnished with majolica floors of Vietri tiles and antiques that the owners have collected since the 17th century. The rooms in the new Casa Palumbo provide a stimulating contrast. The rooms were named after wines from the family's own wine estate and furnished in modern style with magnificent fabrics by Dedar and Rubelli, and designer furniture by Ross Lovegrove and Kravet. In both buildings the most sought-after rooms are those with a balcony or veranda and a sea view. Guests who do not have their own private table should reserve one in the front row of the restaurant terrace and enjoy the immaculate panoramic view of Ravello from there.

**Book to pack: "Palimpsest: A Memoir" by Gore Vidal (the author is a freeman of Ravello).**

**Hotel Palumbo**
Via San Giovanni del Toro 16
84010 Ravello
Italy
Tel. +39 089 857 244
Fax +39 089 858 6084
info@hotelpalumbo.it
www.hotelpalumbo.it
**Open all year round**

| | |
|---|---|
| DIRECTIONS | 50 miles from Naples Airport. |
| RATES | Rooms from 200 €, suites from 350 €, including breakfast. |
| ROOMS | 13 rooms in Palazzo Confalone, 4 in Casa Palumbo. |
| FOOD | At sundown guests have a drink on the terrace of the "Don Pasquale Bar", after which the high-class restaurant "Confalone" serves regional meals. |
| HISTORY | Palazzo Confalone opened in 1875 and has been owned by the Palumbo-Vuilleumier family since then. In 2007 Casa Palumbo was added. |
| X-FACTOR | The idyllic garden with orange and lemon trees. |

## Ein Palast mit Panoramablick

Es ist diese atemberaubende Aussicht, dieses perfekte Panorama, das Ravello so besonders macht: Die kleine Stadt, 350 Meter hoch über der Amalfiküste gelegen, eröffnet einen weiten Blick über Berge und Meer – eingerahmt von alten Steinskulpturen, lila leuchtenden Bougainvilleen oder den Ästen einer Pinie. Dieser Blick ist beim ersten Mal so traumhaft wie nach Jahren, manchmal Magie und oft Inspiration: So schwärmte schon Boccaccio im »Dekameron« von der Schönheit Ravellos, später schrieb D. H. Lawrence hier »Lady Chatterleys Liebhaber« und André Gide »Der Immoralist«. Richard Wagner fand Klingsors Zaubergarten in Ravello und Edvard Grieg Ideen zu »Peer Gynt«. Viele dieser berühmten Gäste wohnten während ihrer Besuche im Hotel Palumbo, das seit mehr als 130 Jahren zu den besten Adressen des Ortes zählt. Herzstück des Hauses ist der historische Palazzo Confalone, in dem die Zimmer klassisch-opulent mit Majolikaböden aus Vietri-Fliesen sowie Antiquitäten ausgestattet sind, welche die Besitzer seit dem 17. Jahrhundert gesammelt haben. Einen spannenden Kontrast setzen die Räume der neuen Casa Palumbo: Sie wurden nach Weinen aus der familieneigenen Winzerei benannt, mit prachtvollen Stoffen von Dedar und Rubelli sowie Designermöbeln von Ross Lovegrove und Kravet modern eingerichtet. Am begehrtesten sind in beiden Gebäuden die Zimmer mit Balkon oder Veranda und Meerblick – wer keinen privaten Freiplatz hat, sollte einen Tisch in der ersten Reihe der Restaurantterrasse reservieren und von dort aus das perfekte Panorama Ravellos genießen.

**Buchtipp: »Palimpsest. Memoiren« von Gore Vidal (der Autor ist Ehrenbürger von Ravello).**

## Palais avec vue

C'est ce panorama à couper le souffle qui fait la particularité de Ravello : située à 350 mètres au-dessus de la côte amalfitaine, la petite ville offre une vaste perspective, encadrée de statues de pierre patinées par les ans, de bougainvillées d'un violet éclatant ou de branches d'un pin, sur les montagnes et la mer. Un spectacle de rêve qui sait conserver sa magie et qui a inspiré plus d'un artiste : la beauté de Ravello ravissait déjà Boccace dans le « Décaméron », plus tard D. H. Lawrence écrira ici « L'Amant de Lady Chatterley » et André Gide « L'Immoraliste ». Richard Wagner y a trouvé le jardin magique de Klingsor et Edvard Grieg des idées pour « Peer Gynt ». Nombre de ces célébrités ont séjourné ici à l'hôtel Palumbo, l'une des meilleures adresses de la ville depuis plus de 130 ans. Le cœur historique de la maison est le Palazzo Confalone, dont les chambres de style classique-opulent sont dotées de carreaux en majolique de Vietri et abritent des antiquités rassemblées par les propriétaires depuis le XVIIe siècle. Ces pièces offrent un contraste saisissant avec les chambres de la nouvelle Casa Palumbo, qui doivent leurs noms aux vins de la propriété et sont aménagées et décorées de manière moderne avec de superbes étoffes de Dedar et Rubelli et des meubles design de Ross Lovegrove et Kravet. Les plus convoitées dans les deux bâtiments sont les chambres avec balcon ou véranda et vue sur la mer – celui qui n'a pas la chance d'y séjourner devrait réserver une table au premier rang de la terrasse du restaurant et jouir paysage sublime qui se déploie sous ses yeux.

**Livre à emporter : « Palimpseste » de Gore Vidal (citoyen d'honneur de Ravello).**

| | | | | |
|---|---|---|---|---|
| ANREISE | 80 km vom Flughafen Neapel entfernt. | | ACCÈS | A 80 km de l'aéroport de Naples. |
| PREISE | Zimmer ab 200 €, Suite ab 350 €, inklusive Frühstück. | | PRIX | Chambre à partir de 200 €, suite à partir de 350 €, petit-déjeuner inclus. |
| ZIMMER | 13 Zimmer im Palazzo Confalone, 4 in der Casa Palumbo. | | CHAMBRES | 13 chambres au Palazzo Confalone, 4 à la Casa Palumbo. |
| KÜCHE | Bei Sonnenuntergang nimmt man einen Drink auf der Terrasse der »Don Pasquale Bar«. Anschließend serviert das edle Restaurant »Confalone« Menüs der Region. | | RESTAURATION | A la tombée du jour, on prend un verre à la terrasse du « Don Pasquale Bar ». Ensuite, l'élégant restaurant « Confalone » propose des plats régionaux. |
| GESCHICHTE | Der Palazzo Confalone wurde 1875 eröffnet und ist seitdem im Besitz der Familie Palumbo-Vuilleumier. 2007 kam die Casa Palumbo dazu. | | HISTOIRE | Le Palazzo Confalone a ouvert ses portes en 1875. Il appartient depuis à la famille Palumbo-Vuilleumier. La Casa Palumbo est venue s'y ajouter en 2007. |
| X-FAKTOR | Der idyllische Garten mit Orangen- und Zitronenbäumen. | | LES « PLUS » | Le jardin idyllique avec ses orangers et ses citronniers. |

# Almost Like Being in Heaven

Villa Cimbrone, Ravello

# Villa Cimbrone, Ravello

**Almost Like Being in Heaven**

When the writer Ferdinand Gregorovius reached Ravello, he found the most beautiful park that he had ever seen around Villa Cimbrone: "In the prettily kept garden the most magnificent show of flowers from countless southern plants blazed all around, in all the glory of the month of July", he enthused in 1861 in his "Siciliana". Today visitors can still stroll around cloisters and beneath bowers, between cypresses, palms and pines, discover hidden wells, temples and grottoes and breathe in the scent of roses. This oasis was created on a spectacular mountain ridge in the early 20th century by Ernest William Beckett, a British dandy later known as Lord Grimthorpe, who had fallen head over heels in love with Villa Cimbrone and transformed it into his private paradise. In accordance with his somewhat eccentric way of life he used a carefree mix of styles. In the house and garden he combined Greek, Roman, Moorish and Venetian elements into a curious but enormously charming work of art. The main building has now become a hotel, provided with every luxury but at the same time fitted out as creatively as in Beckett's day: the best rooms have floors of Vietri tiles, frescoes and open fireplaces. The two large suites have a terrace with a sea view – only the outlook from the belvedere in the park is more beautiful. This was also the opinion of Ferdinand Gregorovius, who wrote: "When looking out from this garden to the siren sea (...), one has a yearning to fly".
**Book to pack: "Siciliana: Wanderings in Naples and Sicily" by Ferdinand Gregorovius.**

| **Hotel Villa Cimbrone** | | |
|---|---|---|
| Via Santa Chiara 26 | DIRECTIONS | 50 miles from Naples Airport. |
| 84010 Ravello | RATES | Rooms from 330 €, suites from 630 €, including breakfast. |
| Italy | ROOMS | 19 rooms and suites. |
| Tel. +39 089 857 459 | FOOD | Many ingredients of the exquisite meals come from the hotel's own organic garden. |
| Fax +39 089 857 777 | | |
| info@villacimbrone.com | HISTORY | The first records of the villa date from the 11th century. Before Beckett bought it in 1904 it belonged to two aristocratic families and Santa Chiara monastery. In 1975 it opened as a bed & breakfast and was extended as a hotel in 1990. |
| www.villacimbrone.com | | |
| **Open from the beginning of** | | |
| **April to the end of December** | X-FACTOR | The park is open to visitors until sunset – in the evenings it is for the exclusive use of hotel guests. |

## Fast wie im Himmel

Als der Schriftsteller Ferdinand Gregorovius nach Ravello kam, fand er rings um die Villa Cimbrone den schönsten Park, den er je gesehen hatte: »In dem zierlich gehaltenen Garten flammte ringsum die köstlichste Blütenpracht ungezählter Gewächse des Südens, in der vollen Glorie des Julimonats«, schwärmte er 1861 in seiner »Siciliana«. Noch heute kann man hier unter Kreuzgängen und Lauben wandeln, zwischen Zypressen, Palmen und Pinien spazieren gehen, versteckte Brunnen, Tempel und Grotten entdecken und den Duft von Rosen einatmen. Angelegt wurde diese Oase auf einem spektakulären Berggrat Anfang des 20. Jahrhunderts von Ernest William Beckett. Der britische Dandy, der später als Lord Grimthorpe berühmt wurde, hatte sich damals unsterblich in die Villa Cimbrone verliebt und sie in sein privates Paradies verwandelt. Seinem etwas exzentrischen Lebensstil entsprechend, mischte er dabei unbekümmert die Stile – in Haus und Garten verband er griechische, römische, maurische sowie venezianische Elemente zu einem kuriosen, aber ungeheuer charmanten Kunstwerk. Inzwischen ist aus dem Hauptgebäude ein Hotel geworden, das mit allem Luxus ausgestattet, aber zugleich so kreativ wie damals gehalten ist: Die besten Zimmer besitzen Vietri-Fliesenböden, Fresken und offene Kamine. Zu den zwei größten Suiten gehören Terrassen mit Meerblick – noch schöner ist die Sicht nur vom Belvedere im Park aus. Dieser Meinung war übrigens auch schon Ferdinand Gregorovius, der schrieb: »Schaut man aus diesem Garten in jenes sirenische Meer (...), dann sehnt man sich zu fliegen.«

**Buchtipp:** »Siciliana. Wanderungen in Neapel und Sicilien« von Ferdinand Gregorovius.

## Comme au ciel

Lorsque l'écrivain Ferdinand Gregorovius arriva à Ravello, il trouva autour de la Villa Cimbrone le parc le plus beau qu'il ait jamais vu : « Dans le plaisant jardin s'enflammait alentour le décor floral le plus exquis d'innombrables plantes du sud dans la gloire du mois de juillet », s'extasie-t-il en 1861. On peut aujourd'hui encore déambuler dans les cloîtres et sous les tonnelles, se promener entre les cyprès, les palmiers et les pins, découvrir des fontaines cachées, des temples et des grottes et humer le parfum des roses. Ce lieu enchanteur a été aménagé au début du XXᵉ siècle sur une arête spectaculaire par Ernest William Beckett. Le dandy britannique, devenu célèbre sous le nom de Lord Grimthorpe, était tombé amoureux fou de la Villa Cimbrone qu'il avait transformée en un paradis à son usage personnel. Fidèle à son mode de vie excentrique, il maria nonchalamment les styles, associant dans la maison et le jardin les éléments grecs, romains, maures et vénitiens pour créer une œuvre d'art singulière, mais ô combien charmante. Aujourd'hui, le bâtiment principal est devenu un hôtel doté de tout le luxe possible, mais qui a su conserver son originalité d'antan : les meilleures chambres abritent des carrelages de Vietri, des fresques murales et des cheminées. Les deux suites les plus vastes sont dotées de terrasses avec vue sur la mer – seule la perspective du belvédère, dans le parc, est plus belle. D'ailleurs, Ferdinand Gregorovius était bien de cet avis lorsqu'il écrivait : « Si l'on regarde la mer sirénique de ce jardin (...), on a envie de voler. »

**Livre à emporter :** « Promenades en Italie et en Corse » de Ferdinand Gregorovius.

| | | | | |
|---|---|---|---|---|
| ANREISE | 80 km vom Flughafen Neapel entfernt. | ACCÈS | A 80 km de l'aéroport de Naples. |
| PREISE | Zimmer ab 330 €, Suite ab 630 €, inklusive Frühstück. | PRIX | Chambre à partir de 330 €, suite à partir de 630 €, petit-déjeuner inclus. |
| ZIMMER | 19 Zimmer und Suiten. | CHAMBRES | 19 chambres et suites. |
| KÜCHE | Viele Zutaten für die exquisiten Menüs stammen aus dem hoteleigenen Bio-Garten. | RESTAURATION | De nombreux ingrédients des plats délicieux proviennent du jardin bio de l'hôtel. |
| GESCHICHTE | Die Villa wurde im 11. Jahrhundert erstmals urkundlich erwähnt. Ehe sie 1904 von Beckett gekauft wurde, gehörte sie zwei Adelsfamilien sowie zum Kloster Santa Chiara. 1975 eröffnete sie als Bed & Breakfast und wurde 1990 zum Hotel erweitert. | HISTOIRE | La villa est mentionnée pour la première fois au XIᵉ siècle. Elle a appartenu à deux familles nobles, au couvent Santa Chiara et à Beckett en 1904. Bed & Breakfast en 1975, elle devient hôtel en 1990. |
| X-FAKTOR | Bis Sonnenuntergang ist der Park für Besucher geöffnet – abends gehört er exklusiv den Hotelgästen. | LES « PLUS » | Le parc est fermé au public après le coucher du soleil, il appartient alors aux clients de l'hôtel. |

# An Italian Idyll
## Palazzo Belmonte, Salerno

# Palazzo Belmonte, Salerno

**An Italian Idyll**

It is a challenge not to feel intimidated by the grandezza of Rome, the glamour of the Amalfi coast and the temperament of Naples – but the Cilento calmly rises to the task. This coastal region in Campania remains as down to earth today as it was centuries ago, and gives priority to the tranquillity of country life amidst unspoiled natural beauty rather than any tourist bustle. Of course its residents are proud of sights such as the Temple of Paestum, which Goethe praised so highly. But instead of advertising these things in multimedia marketing campaigns, the residents allow visitors to discover them in passing – just like the wonderful food (the authentic buffalo mozzarella and the original hand-twisted fusilli pasta come from Cilento) and the warmth of the locals. One of the best hosts here is Angelo Granito Pignatelli di Belmonte: in Palazzo Belmonte, where his ancestors once received the kings of Italy and Spain to hunt wild boar, this prince from an ancient aristocratic family now welcomes guests and introduces them to the beauty of his homeland with all his charm and charisma. In the elegant rooms, at the pool or on the private beach, in the restaurant, on the massage table or during a walk with the master of the house – everything can be enjoyed in peace here. A holiday in Cilento is as good as it gets – but that goes without saying.

**Book to pack:** "Italian Journey" by Johann Wolfgang von Goethe.

**Palazzo Belmonte**
Via Flavio Gioia 25
84072 Santa Maria di Castellabate
Italy
Tel. +39 0974 960 211
Fax +39 0974 961 150
info@palazzobelmonte.com
www.palazzobelmonte.com
**Open all year round (from December
to May only as bed & breakfast)**

| | |
|---|---|
| DIRECTIONS | On the coast of Campania, 80 miles south of Naples Airport. |
| RATES | Rooms from 186 €, suites from 316 €, including breakfast. |
| ROOMS | 53 rooms, suites and apartments. |
| FOOD | Mediterranean meals with lots of fish; best enjoyed on the panorama terrace. |
| HISTORY | Palazzo Belmonte dates from the 17th century and is still owned by the original family (they live in a private wing). |
| X-FACTOR | Villa Belmonte in the garden with especially quiet rooms and a sea view. |

## Ein italienisches Idyll

Sich von der Grandezza Roms, dem Glamour der Amalfiküste und dem Temperament Neapels nicht einschüchtern
zu lassen, ist eine Herausforderung – doch der Cilento
meistert sie gänzlich ungerührt. Die Küstenregion in
Kampanien zeigt sich noch heute so bodenständig wie vor
Jahrhunderten und gibt dem unaufgeregten Landleben
inmitten einer ursprünglichen Natur den Vorzug vor jeg-
lichem Touristentrubel. Selbstverständlich ist man stolz
auf Sehenswürdigkeiten wie die griechischen Tempel von
Paestum, von denen Goethe so sehr schwärmte. Doch man
bewirbt sie nicht mit multimedialen Marketingkampagnen,
sondern lässt sie Besucher en passant entdecken – ebenso
wie die wunderbare Küche (aus dem Cilento stammen
sowohl der echte Büffelmozzarella als auch die originalen,
von Hand gedrehten Fusilli-Nudeln) und die Herzlichkeit
der Einheimischen. Zu den besten Gastgebern zählt dabei
Angelo Granito Pignatelli di Belmonte: Im Palazzo Belmonte,
in dem seine Vorfahren einst die Könige von Italien und
Spanien zur Wildschweinjagd empfingen, heißt der Fürst aus
altem Adel heute Fremde willkommen und bringt ihnen mit
ebenso viel Charme wie Charisma die Schönheiten seiner
Heimat nahe. Ob in den eleganten Zimmern, am Pool oder
Privatstrand, am Restauranttisch, auf der Massageliege oder
beim Spaziergang mit dem Hausherrn – hier lässt sich alles
in aller Ruhe genießen; so selbstverständlich schön können
nur Ferien im Cilento sein.

**Buchtipp: »Italienische Reise« von Johann Wolfgang von Goethe.**

## Idylle à l'italienne

La gloire de Rome, le glamour de la côte amalfitaine et le
tempérament de Naples ont de quoi impressionner, mais le
Cilento ne se laisse pas du tout intimider. La région littorale
de la Campanie a gardé la simplicité qui la caractérise depuis
des siècles et préfère le calme de la campagne dans des paysages originels au tumulte des villes bondées de touristes.
On est évidemment fier du patrimoine, par exemple du
temple grec de Paestum qui ravissait Goethe. Mais pas question de le présenter à l'aide de campagnes de marketing
multimédia – on laisse les visiteurs le découvrir au gré de
leur séjour, comme ils découvriront la cuisine savoureuse
(c'est du Cilento que proviennent l'authentique mozarelle au
lait de bufflesse et les fusilli originaux, roulés à la main) et le
caractère chaleureux des habitants. Angelo Granito Pignatelli
di Belmonte, est l'un de ces hôtes privilégiés : dans le palais
de Belmonte où ses ancêtres recevaient autrefois les rois
d'Italie et d'Espagne venus chasser le sanglier, le prince
accueille aujourd'hui des étrangers et leur fait connaître les
beautés de son pays avec autant de charisme que de séduction.
Que ce soit dans les chambres élégantes, au bord de la piscine
ou sur la plage privée, à table au restaurant, sur le lit de
massage ou en promenade avec le maître de maison – on
peut jouir ici de tout en toute quiétude. Seules des vacances
à Cilento peuvent être aussi naturellement belles.

**Livre à emporter : « Voyage en Italie » de Johann Wolfgang von Goethe.**

| ANREISE | An der Küste Kampaniens gelegen, 130 km südlich des Flughafens von Neapel. |
|---|---|
| PREISE | Zimmer ab 186 €, Suite ab 316 €, inklusive Frühstück. |
| ZIMMER | 53 Zimmer, Suiten und Apartments. |
| KÜCHE | Mediterrane Menüs mit viel Fisch; am schönsten serviert auf der Panoramaterrasse. |
| GESCHICHTE | Der Palazzo Belmonte stammt aus dem 17. Jahrhundert und ist noch heute in Familienbesitz (der Eigentümer bewohnt einen privaten Flügel). |
| X-FAKTOR | Die Villa Belmonte im Garten mit besonders ruhigen Zimmern und Meerblick. |

| ACCÈS | Sur la côte de Campanie, à 130 km de l'aéroport de Naples. |
|---|---|
| PRIX | Chambre à partir de 186 €, suite à partir de 316 €, petit-déjeuner inclus. |
| CHAMBRES | 53 chambres, suites et appartements. |
| RESTAURATION | Cuisine méditerranéenne riche en poisson ; la terrasse panoramique est le plus bel endroit pour la déguster. |
| HISTOIRE | Le Palazzo Belmonte date du XVIIe siècle et est encore aux mains de la famille (le propriétaire loge dans une aile privée). |
| LES « PLUS » | La Villa Belmonte, au jardin, abrite des chambres particulièrement calmes avec vue sur la mer. |

# Ancient Heritage Rediscovered
Sextantio Le Grotte della Civita, Matera

# Sextantio Le Grotte della Civita, Matera

**Ancient Heritage Rediscovered**

It is hard to say where the rock stops and the town starts: on the steep slope where Matera lies, stone fuses with stone to form a surface that is glacier-grey under a cloudy sky and shimmers in pastel tones when the sun shines. Only on the crown of the hill can the outlines of individual houses be made out, with the silhouette of the tower rising above them. The reason for this seamless transition between architecture and nature is the element that binds them together – the legendary caves of tufa stone whose origins go back to the Bronze Age and thus make Matera one of the oldest towns in the world. Until the mid-20th century the "sassi" (rocks) were inhabited, but then were closed on hygienic grounds and decayed. It was not until the 1980s that Matera rediscovered its caves and began to restore them – with such success that they are now listed as a World Heritage Site. Recently a few caves became habitable once again – at least for guests at Sextantio's "albergo diffuso" Le Grotte della Civita. The Sextantio group brought to Matera its vision of conserving heritage that had almost been forgotten, of monuments authentically restored and at the same time incorporating a modern sensibility. Margareta Berg and Daniele Kihlgren created a hotel of ultimate simplicity and almost unreal beauty, where you sometimes feel like an actor on a film set, sometimes like a researcher at a dig – and always in a state of suspension between past and present. Here, below the earth, the ages seem to fuse, as imperceptibly as the rock and the town outside.

**Book to pack: "Christ Stopped at Eboli" by Carlo Levi.**

| | |
|---|---|
| **Sextantio Le Grotte della Civita** | |
| Via Civita 28 | |
| Sasso Barisano | |
| 75100 Matera | |
| Italy | |
| Tel. +39 0835 332 744 | |
| Fax +39 0835 337 331 | |
| info@sassidimatera.com | |
| www.sassidimatera.com | |
| **Open all year round** | |

| | |
|---|---|
| DIRECTIONS | Matera is situated in the Basilicata region in southern Italy; 40 miles from Bari Airport. |
| RATES | From 225 € per night, including breakfast. |
| ROOMS | 18 caves, each with its own bathroom. |
| FOOD | Breakfast is served in an old rock church – bread, butter, honey and jam come exclusively from the town and region. |
| HISTORY | Opened in May 2009. |
| X-FACTOR | The fantastic lighting with candles and indirect illumination. |

## Ein altes Erbe, neu entdeckt

Es ist schwer zu sagen, wo der Fels aufhört und wo die Stadt anfängt: Unten am Steilhang von Matera verschmelzen Stein und Stein zu einer Fläche, die bei bewölktem Himmel gletschergrau und im Sonnenschein pastellfarben schimmert. Erst auf der Kuppe des Hügels lassen sich die Umrisse einzelner Häuser ausmachen, gekrönt von der Silhouette des Turms. Dass Natur und Architektur so nahtlos ineinander übergehen, liegt an ihrem Bindeglied – den legendären Tuffsteinhöhlen, deren Ursprünge bis in die Bronzezeit zurückreichen und die Matera damit zu einer der ältesten Städte der Welt machen. Bis Mitte des 20. Jahrhunderts waren die »sassi« (Felsen) bewohnt, ehe sie aus hygienischen Gründen geschlossen wurden und verfielen. Erst in den 1980ern besann sich Matera wieder auf seine Grotten und begann, sie zu sanieren – so erfolgreich, dass sie heute auf der Liste der Weltkulturerbe stehen. Seit Kurzem sind einige Höhlen auch erneut bewohnbar; zumindest für die Gäste von Sextantios »albergo diffuso«, Le Grotte della Civita. Die Sextantio-Gruppe hat ihre Vision vom Bewahren beinahe vergessenen Kulturguts, von originalgetreu restaurierten und zugleich modern wirkenden Denkmälern nach Matera gebracht, wo Margareta Berg und Daniele Kihlgren ein ultimativ schlichtes, fast unwirklich schönes Hotel geschaffen haben. Man fühlt sich manchmal wie ein Schauspieler am Filmset, manchmal wie ein Forscher am Ausgrabungsort – und immer wie im Schwebezustand zwischen Geschichte und Gegenwart. Die Zeiten scheinen hier unter der Erde zusammenzufließen; so unmerklich wie draußen der Fels und die Stadt.

**Buchtipp: »Christus kam nur bis Eboli« von Carlo Levi.**

## Le patrimoine redécouvert

Où s'arrête la falaise et où commence la ville ? C'est difficile à dire : en bas, sur la pente escarpée de Matera, la surface des pierres ressemble à un glacier gris lorsque le ciel est nuageux, et elle a des tons bleu pastel au soleil. On ne distingue les contours de quelques maisons que lorsqu'on a atteint le sommet de la colline sur lequel est posée une tour. Si la nature et l'architecture font si bon ménage, c'est grâce aux légendaires grottes de tuf, dont l'origine remonte à l'âge de bronze et qui font donc de Matera l'une des plus anciennes villes du monde. Les « sassi », les cavités naturelles du rocher, ont abrité des troglodytes jusqu'au milieu du XXe siècle ; elles ont ensuite été fermées pour des raisons de salubrité. Et puis, au cours des années 1980, Matera s'est souvenue de ses grottes et a commencé à les réhabiliter, et ce avec tant de succès qu'elles sont aujourd'hui inscrites sur la liste du patrimoine mondial. Depuis peu, certaines grottes sont à nouveau habitables, du moins pour les hôtes de Sextantio « albergo diffuso » Le Grotte della Civita. Le groupe Sextantio a apporté à Matera sa vision de préservation d'un patrimoine presque oublié, de restauration fidèle à l'original mariée à une sensibilité moderne, créant en collaboration avec Margareta Berg et Daniele Kihlgren un hôtel on ne peut plus sobre, d'une beauté presque irréelle. On se sent parfois comme un acteur sur le plateau de tournage, parfois comme un archéologue sur un lieu de fouilles, et toujours entre le passé et le présent qui semblent ici fusionner sous la terre, de manière aussi imperceptible que la roche et la ville au-dessus.

**Livre à emporter : « Le Christ s'est arrêté à Éboli » de Carlo Levi.**

| | | | |
|---|---|---|---|
| ANREISE | Matera liegt in der süditalienischen Region Basilikata, 65 km vom Flughafen Bari entfernt. | ACCÈS | Matera est située dans la région de Basilicate, dans le sud de l'Italie ; à 65 km de l'aéroport de Bari. |
| PREISE | Übernachtung ab 225 €, inklusive Frühstück. | PRIX | Nuit à partir de 225 €, petit-déjeuner inclus. |
| ZIMMER | 18 Höhlen mit jeweils eigenem Bad. | CHAMBRES | 18 grottes avec salle de bains. |
| KÜCHE | Frühstück wird in einer alten Steinkirche serviert – Brot, Butter, Honig und Marmelade stammen ausschließlich aus der Stadt und Region. | RESTAURATION | Le petit-déjeuner est servi dans une ancienne église rupestre – le pain, le beurre, le miel et les confitures proviennent de la région. |
| GESCHICHTE | Im Mai 2009 eröffnet. | HISTOIRE | Ouvert en mai 2009. |
| X-FAKTOR | Die fantastische Beleuchtung mit Kerzen und indirektem Licht. | LES « PLUS » | L'éclairage fantastique à la bougie avec lumière indirecte. |

# Welcome to the White City
La Sommità, Ostuni

# La Sommità, Ostuni

**Welcome to the White City**

White is the sum of all the colours, the symbol for peace, purity and innocence in Western cultures. They say that it is a word known to the Inuit in about two hundred variations. White is a phenomenon – universal, age-old and so timeless that it never goes out of fashion. For proof of this go to Ostuni, which even bears this idea in its name: it is known far beyond the borders of Apulia as "città bianca", "white city". Built on the crown of a hill girdled by olive trees, its close-standing houses were once limewashed in shining white – seen from a distance Ostuni still looks like an outsize egg-white meringue, and to stroll through its pretty town centre is to discover a bright labyrinth of lanes and alleys. You need a good sense of direction to find the way to Relais La Sommità, a historic palazzo that Alessandro Agrati has transformed into a completely white hotel, in keeping with the style of the town. Agrati, founder of the Italian lifestyle brand Culti, has furnished the vaulted rooms entirely with minimalist products from his label, installed ingenious lighting and selected fragrances and music to match. To make sure that the ensemble does not look like a formal showroom there are palm-shaded loggias, a Spanish garden with orange trees and, of course, the panorama from the windows: the view across the white city is breathtaking and extends all the way to the deep blue sea.

**Book to pack: "Involuntary Witness" by Gianrico Carofiglio.**

**Relais La Sommità**
Via Scipione Petrarolo 7
72017 Ostuni
Italy
Tel. +39 0831 305 925
Fax +39 0831 306 729
info@lasommita.it
www.lasommita.it
**Open all year round**

| | |
|---|---|
| DIRECTIONS | 62 miles from Bari Airport, 31 miles from Brindisi Airport. |
| RATES | Rooms from 300 €, including breakfast. |
| ROOMS | 5 rooms and 9 suites. |
| FOOD | The restaurant "Profumo" serves aromatic Apulian dishes; there is also a vinoteca. |
| HISTORY | The 16th-century building opened as a hotel in 2004. |
| X-FACTOR | The outstanding, atmospheric spa with a hammam easily makes up for the fact that the hotel has no pool. |

## Willkommen in der weißen Stadt

Weiß ist die Summe aller Farben. In westlichen Kulturen das Symbol für Frieden, Reinheit und Unschuld. Man sagt, dass die Inuit dieses Wort in rund zweihundert Variationen kennen. Weiß ist ein Phänomen – universell, uralt und so zeitlos, dass es nie aus der Mode kommt. Das beweist auch der Ort Ostuni, der den Begriff sogar im Namen trägt – er ist als »città bianca«, als »weiße Stadt« weit über Apuliens Grenzen hinaus bekannt. Die Häuser der Stadt, die auf der Kuppe eines mit Olivenbäumen umkränzten Hügels errichtet sind, wurden einst mit Kalk strahlend weiß getüncht und eng aneinandergebaut – aus der Ferne betrachtet, sieht Ostuni noch heute wie ein überdimensionales Eischnee-baiser aus, und wer durch das pittoreske Zentrum spaziert, erkundet ein lichtes Labyrinth von Gassen und Gässchen. Man braucht einen guten Orientierungssinn, um hier zum Relais La Sommità zu finden – einem historischen Palazzo, den Alessandro Agrati ganz im Stil der Stadt zu einem Hotel ganz in Weiß verwandelt hat. Der Gründer der italienischen Lifestylemarke Culti hat die Räume unter alten Gewölbe-decken ausschließlich mit den minimalistischen Möbeln seines Labels ausgestattet, raffiniert beleuchtet (am schönsten sind die Suiten mit Oberlichtern) und die dazu passenden Düfte und Musiktitel ausgewählt. Dafür, dass das Ganze nicht wie ein steifer Showroom wirkt, sorgen Loggien unter Palmen, ein spanischer Garten mit Orangenbäumen und natürlich der Blick aus den Fenstern: Die Sicht über die weiße Stadt ist atemberaubend und reicht bis zum Meer – ganz in Blau.

**Buchtipp: »Reise in die Nacht« von Gianrico Carofiglio.**

## Bienvenue dans la cité blanche

Le blanc est la somme de toutes les couleurs, le symbole de la paix, de la pureté et de l'innocence dans la civilisation occidentale. On dit que les Inuits ont environ deux cents mots à leur disposition pour le désigner. Le blanc est un phénomène universel, remontant à la nuit des temps et qui ne risque pas de passer de mode. Ostuni, la « città bianca » connue bien au-delà des frontières des Pouilles, en est la preuve. Edifiées côte à côte au sommet d'une colline plantée d'oliviers, ses maisons blanchies à la chaux retiennent la lumière – vue de loin, Ostuni évoque une énorme meringue, et celui qui se promène dans son centre pittoresque doit explorer un labyrinthe de ruelles. Il faut être doué d'un bon sens de l'orientation pour trouver ici le Relais La Sommità, un palais historique qu'Alessandro Agrati a transformé en hôtel et adapté au style de la ville en le peignant en blanc. Le fondateur de la marque life-style Culti a aménagé les pièces voûtées exclusivement avec les meubles minimalistes de sa marque, les a éclairées de manière raffinée (les suites avec éclairage zénithal sont les plus belles) et sélectionné les parfums d'ambiance et les titres de musique correspondants. Cela pourrait ressembler à un show-room guindé, mais ce n'est pas le cas grâce aux loggias sous les palmiers, un jardin d'orangers espagnol et, évidemment, la vue à couper le souffle sur la ville blanche qui rejoint la mer toute bleue.

**Livre à emporter : « Le Passé est une terre étrangère » de Gianrico Carofiglio.**

| ANREISE | 100 km vom Flughafen Bari entfernt, 50 km vom Flug-hafen Brindisi. |
|---|---|
| PREISE | Zimmer ab 300 €, inklusive Frühstück. |
| ZIMMER | 5 Zimmer und 9 Suiten. |
| KÜCHE | Im Restaurant »Profumo« werden aromatische apulische Gerichte serviert; zudem gibt es eine Vinoteca. |
| GESCHICHTE | Der Bau aus dem 16. Jahrhundert wurde 2004 als Hotel eröffnet. |
| X-FAKTOR | Das stimmungsvolle und ausgezeichnete Spa mit Hamam lässt schnell vergessen, dass das Hotel keinen Pool besitzt. |

| ACCÈS | A 100 km de l'aéroport de Bari, à 50 km de celui de Brindisi. |
|---|---|
| PRIX | Chambre à partir de 300 €, petit-déjeuner inclus. |
| CHAMBRES | 5 chambres et 9 suites. |
| RESTAURATION | Le « Profumo » sert des plats aromatiques de la cuisine des Pouilles ; une vinothèque est réservée aux dégustations. |
| HISTOIRE | Le bâtiment du XVIe siècle est un hôtel depuis 2004. |
| LES « PLUS » | Le spa avec hammam, qui fait vite oublier que l'hôtel n'a pas de piscine. |

# Good All Round
Villa Cenci, Cisternino

# Villa Cenci, Cisternino

**Good All Round**

They were too poor to own their own plot of land, but they knew a little trick that made it possible to be house owners all the same: the Apulian peasants of the 13th to 17th centuries built their trulli, simple round houses with a cone-shaped roof, solely from stones that lay in the fields and without any mortar at all. In this way their habitations could be dismantled in the twinkling of an eye if the authorities made checks, and reconstructed as soon as the danger was past. Once accommodation for times of need, today they are national monuments: the trulli are among the most coveted and famous buildings in Apulia, and the radiant whitewashed trulli of Alberobello have even been listed as Unesco World Heritage since 1996. Just under 12 miles east of the town one of the loveliest trulli hotels welcomes its guests: Villa Cenci is an old country estate that has been restored both expertly and tastefully, and in addition to guest rooms in the main building possesses nine rooms in trulli – an indispensable feature, of course, in this place. The only reminder of past austerity is the shape of the houses; apart from that modern times have arrived, with sunshades, four-poster beds, TV and air conditioning. And the owners of Villa Cenci are not short of land: all around the buildings lie 32 acres of natural beauty, of which there is a wonderful view from the pool. The fruit and vegetables that grow on the land are the basis for the fine organic cuisine, which is served in the hotel restaurant or right in front of the trulli.

**Book to pack: "I'm not Scared" by Niccolò Ammaniti.**

| | |
|---|---|
| **Villa Cenci Relais Masseria** | |
| Strada Provinciale per Ceglie Messapica | |
| 72014 Cisternino | |
| Italy | |
| Tel. +39 080 4448 208 | |
| info@villacenci.it | |
| www.villacenci.it | |
| **Open from the beginning of** | |
| **March to the end of December** | |

| | |
|---|---|
| DIRECTIONS | In Valle d'Itria, 6 miles from the sea and 55 miles from Bari Airport. |
| RATES | Rooms from 160 €, suites from 250 €, including breakfast. |
| ROOMS | 9 rooms in trulli, 11 rooms and suites in the masseria. |
| FOOD | The open-air breakfast is legendary; dinner and lunch are cooked to traditional Apulian recipes. |
| HISTORY | The estate was converted into a country hotel in 1985. The elegant Relais has existed in its present form since 2007. |
| X-FACTOR | The little spa with a sauna and hammam. |

## Eine runde Sache

Sie waren zu arm, um ein eigenes Stück Land zu besitzen – doch dank eines kleinen Tricks konnten sie dennoch ein Haus ihr Eigen nennen: Die apulischen Bauern des 13. bis 17. Jahrhunderts bauten ihre Trulli, schlichte Rundhäuser mit kegelförmigem Dach, nur aus Steinen aufs Feld und verzichteten ganz auf Mörtel. So ließen sich die Behausungen im Fall einer behördlichen Kontrolle im Handumdrehen abbauen und wieder neu errichten, sobald die Gefahr vorbei war. Heute sind aus den einstigen Notunterkünften Nationaldenkmäler geworden: Die Trulli zählen zu den begehrtesten und berühmtesten Bauten Apuliens – die strahlend weiß getünchten Trulli von Alberobello stehen seit 1996 sogar auf der Weltkulturerbe-Liste der UNESCO. Knapp 20 Kilometer östlich der Stadt wartet eines der schönsten Trulli-Hotels auf Gäste: Die Villa Cenci ist ein altes Landgut, das mit ebenso viel Sachverstand wie Stil restauriert wurde und neben Gästezimmern im Hauptgebäude neun Räume in Trulli besitzt – diese sind hier natürlich ein Muss. An die karge Vergangenheit erinnert dabei nur noch die Form der Häuser; ansonsten sind mit Sonnensegel, Himmelbett, Fernseher sowie Klimaanlage moderne Zeiten eingezogen. Auch an Land mangelt es den Besitzern der Villa Cenci nicht: Rund um das Anwesen dehnen sich 13 Hektar herrlichste Natur aus, über die man vom Pool aus einen wunderschönen Blick hat. Das Obst und Gemüse, welches auf dem Grundstück gedeiht, ist Basis für die feine Bio-Küche des Hotels, die im Restaurant serviert wird – oder direkt vor der Tür der Trulli.

**Buchtipp: »Die Herren des Hügels« von Niccolò Ammaniti.**

## Tout beau, tout rond

Trop pauvres pour acheter un peu de terre, ils étaient assez malins pour avoir une maison bien à eux : du XIII$^e$ au XVII$^e$ siècle, les paysans des Pouilles bâtirent dans les champs des trulli, de sobres maisons rondes au toit conique construites sans mortier, à l'aide de galets. Si quelqu'un venait contrôler, ils pouvaient démonter leurs habitations en un rien de temps et les reconstruire dès que le danger était passé. Ces logements provisoires sont devenus des monuments nationaux et font aujourd'hui partie des constructions les plus convoitées et les plus célèbres des Pouilles – les trulli d'un blanc éclatant d'Alberobello sont même classés depuis 1996 au patrimoine mondial de l'UNESCO. L'un des plus beaux ensembles de trulli attend ses hôtes à une vingtaine de kilomètres à l'est de la ville : la villa Cenci est un ancien domaine rural restauré avec style par des experts en la matière. A côté des chambres situées dans le bâtiment principal, elle possède neuf pièces dans des trulli – un must dans cette région. Seule la forme des maisons évoque encore le dénuement des habitants de jadis ; sinon, la modernité a fait son apparition, apportant des tauds de soleil, des lits à baldaquin, la télévision et la climatisation. Les propriétaires de la villa Cenci ne manquent pas de terrain non plus : 13 hectares de nature se déploient autour de la propriété, et la vue que l'on en a de la piscine est sublime. Les fruits et légumes cultivés sur place sont la base de la cuisine bio raffinée, proposée au restaurant de l'hôtel – ou directement à la porte des trulli.

**Livre à emporter : « Je n'ai pas peur » de Niccolò Ammaniti.**

| | | | |
|---|---|---|---|
| ANREISE | Im Valle d'Itria gelegen, 10 km vom Meer entfernt. Die Distanz zum Flughafen Bari beträgt 90 km. | ACCÈS | Dans le Valle d'Itria, à 10 km de la mer et à 90 km de l'aéroport de Bari. |
| PREISE | Zimmer ab 160 €, Suite ab 250 €, inklusive Frühstück. | PRIX | Chambre à partir de 160 €, suite à partir 250 €, petit-déjeuner inclus. |
| ZIMMER | 9 Zimmer in Trulli, 11 Zimmer und Suiten in der Masseria. | CHAMBRES | 9 chambres dans les trulli, 11 chambres et suites dans la masseria. |
| KÜCHE | Das Frühstück unter freiem Himmel ist legendär; mittags und abends wird nach traditionellen apulischen Rezepten gekocht. | RESTAURATION | Le petit-déjeuner en plein air est réputé ; midi et soir, on propose des recettes locales traditionnelles. |
| GESCHICHTE | Das Gut wurde 1985 in ein Landhotel verwandelt. Das elegante Relais in seiner heutigen Form besteht seit 2007. | HISTOIRE | Le domaine a été transformé en hôtel de campagne en 1985. Le relais élégant sous sa forme actuelle existe depuis 2007. |
| X-FAKTOR | Das kleine Spa mit Sauna und Hamam. | LES « PLUS » | Le petit spa avec sauna et hammam. |

# Timeless Beauty
Relais Histó S. Pietro sul Mar Piccolo, Taranto

# Relais Histó S. Pietro sul Mar Piccolo, Taranto

**Open all year round**

**Timeless Beauty**

There is no lack of legends about the origins of the city of Taranto. The pragmatic version quite simply attributes its foundation to Heracles. There is a more colourful story about Taras, a demi-god and son of Poseidon, who was saved by a dolphin after a storm at sea, rode to land on the dolphin's back and established the settlement. And the inhabitants' favourite tale is the myth of Phalantus the Spartan, whom the oracle at Delphi prophesied would conquer a new place as soon as rain fell when all around was sunny. Phalanthus set out on a voyage, and one day when he saw his wife Ethra (the Greek word for "joyful") crying, had the solution to the riddle – he anchored and laid the foundation stone of Taranto on the nearest shore. Those who would like to immerse themselves in history more deeply and in surroundings to match should book a room in the Relais Histó, a medieval masseria that houses a stylish hotel today. Alessandro Agrati, who also designed Relais La Sommità, preserved the traditional structure and materials of the estate during restoration and combined it with modern Culti furniture in shades of cream, grey and brown – historic and contemporary elements in wonderful equilibrium. It is necessary to book early for a room with a sea view, but there is also much to be said for the ones that look out onto orange trees. The view and the ambience are just right in the restaurant and around the pool – the opening of this hotel has probably put an end once and for all to tears on a sunny day.

**Book to pack: "The Myths and Legends of Ancient Greece and Rome" by E. M. Berens.**

**Relais Histó S. Pietro sul Mar Piccolo**
Via Santandrea Circummarpiccolo
74100 Taranto
Italy
Tel./Fax +39 099 472 1188
info@histo.it
www.relaishisto.it
**Open all year round**

| | |
|---|---|
| DIRECTIONS | On the lagoon 6 miles outside Taranto, 40 miles from Brindisi Airport. |
| RATES | Rooms from 170 €, suites from 420 €, including breakfast. |
| ROOMS | 39 rooms and 7 suites in the former monastery Antica Sorgente and in the Zona Nobile wing. |
| FOOD | The restaurant "Lanternaia" on the premises of a former olive press serves Apulian specialities. |
| HISTORY | In the late 14th century the masseria, which was later used as a monastery, was built in the ruins of a Roman villa. The hotel opened in 2008. |
| X-FACTOR | The new spa in the style of Roman baths. |

## Zeitlos schön

An Legenden über ihre Entstehung mangelt es der Stadt
Tarent nicht: Die pragmatische Version schreibt die Gründung
schlicht und einfach Herakles zu. Etwas farbenprächtiger ist
die Geschichte von Taras, Halbgott und Sohn Poseidons, der
nach einem Seesturm von einem Delfin gerettet wurde, auf
dessen Rücken an Land ritt und dort eine Siedlung errichtete.
Und am liebsten erzählen die Bewohner die Sage von dem
Spartaner Phalantus, dem das Orakel von Delphi vorherge-
sagt hatte, er werde einen neuen Ort erobern, sobald es bei
heiterem Himmel regnen werde. Phalantus brach zu einer
Schiffsreise auf, und als er eines Tages seine Frau Aithra
(griechisch für »die Heitere«) weinen sah, schien das Rätsel
gelöst – er warf den Anker und legte am nächsten Ufer den
Grundstein Tarents. Wer tiefer und in passendem Ambiente
in die Historie eintauchen möchte, bucht am besten das
Relais Histó – eine mittelalterliche Masseria, die heute ein
stilvolles Hotel beherbergt. Alessandro Agrati, der auch das
Relais La Sommità entworfen hat, hat bei der Renovierung
des Anwesens dessen traditionelle Strukturen und Materialien
erhalten und sie mit modernem Culti-Mobiliar in Creme-,
Grau- und Braunnuancen kombiniert – eine wunderbare
Balance zwischen Geschichte und Gegenwart. Die Zimmer
mit Meerblick muss man rechtzeitig reservieren, doch auch
der Blick aus den Räumen über den Orangenbäumen ist
traumhaft. Aussicht und Ambiente stimmen im Restaurant
ebenso wie am Pool – Tränen bei heiterem Himmel dürften
in Tarent also spätestens seit der Eröffnung dieses Hotels
passé sein.

**Buchtipp: »Sagen des klassischen Altertums« von Gustav Schwab.**

## D'hier et d'aujourd'hui

Les légendes décrivant la naissance de Tarente ne manquent
pas, la version la plus pragmatique attribuant tout simplement sa fondation à Héraclès. Plus colorée est celle qui nous
montre Tara, fils de Poséidon et d'une nymphe, pris dans une
tempête en mer. Sauvé par un dauphin, il le chevauchera
jusqu'à la terre ferme où il fondera une colonie. Mais la
légende que les habitants racontent le plus volontiers est
celle du Spartiate Phalantus, à qui l'oracle de Delphes avait
prédit qu'il conquerrait un nouvel endroit dès qu'il verrait
« pleuvoir par un temps serein ». Phalantus entreprit un
voyage en Italie et comprit l'énigme, le jour où il vit pleurer
sa femme Ethra (en grec, la sereine) – il jeta l'ancre et posa
sur la rive la plus proche la première pierre de Tarente. Les
amateurs d'histoire appréciant le cadre adapté devraient
réserver une chambre au Relais Histó – une masseria médié-
vale qui abrite aujourd'hui un hôtel élégant. Alessandro Agrati
– il a aussi conçu le Relais La Sommità – a su conserver ses
structures et matériaux traditionnels, les combinant à un
mobilier moderne de Culti en tons crème, gris et bruns – un
superbe équilibre entre le passé et le présent. Les chambres
avec vue sur la mer doivent être réservées à temps, mais
la vue de celles qui donnent sur les orangers n'est pas à
dédaigner non plus. Que l'on se trouve au restaurant ou à
la piscine, la vue et l'ambiance sont garanties. A Tarente,
depuis l'ouverture de l'hôtel, les larmes ne devraient donc
plus couler par un ciel serein.

**Livre à emporter : « Mythologie grecque et romaine » de Pierre
Commelin.**

| | | | |
|---|---|---|---|
| ANREISE | An der Lagune 10 km außerhalb von Tarent gelegen, 65 km vom Flughafen Brindisi entfernt. | ACCÈS | Sur la lagune, à 10 km de Tarente, à 65 km de l'aéroport de Brindisi. |
| PREISE | Zimmer ab 170 €, Suite ab 420 €, inklusive Frühstück. | PRIX | Chambre à partir de 170 €, suite à partir de 420 €, petit-déjeuner inclus. |
| ZIMMER | 39 Zimmer und 7 Suiten im einstigen Klosterbereich Antica Sorgente und im Flügel Zona Nobile. | CHAMBRES | 39 chambres et 7 suites dans l'ancien monastère Antica Sorgente et dans l'aile Zona Nobile. |
| KÜCHE | Das Lokal »Lanternaia« in einer ehemaligen Olivenpresse serviert apulische Spezialitäten. | RESTAURATION | La « Lanternaia », dans un ancien pressoir à olives, propose des spécialités des Pouilles. |
| GESCHICHTE | Aus den Ruinen einer römischen Villa entstand Ende des 14. Jahrhunderts die Masseria, die später als Kloster diente. Das Hotel eröffnete 2008. | HISTOIRE | La masseria, devenue un monastère, a vu le jour à la fin du XIVᵉ siècle des ruines d'une villa romaine. L'hôtel a ouvert ses portes en 2008. |
| X-FAKTOR | Das neue Spa im Stil römischer Bäder. | LES « PLUS » | Le nouveau spa qui s'inspire des thermes romains. |

# A Remarkable Collection
Convento di Santa Maria di Costantinopoli, Marittima di Diso

# Convento di Santa Maria di Costantinopoli, Marittima di Diso

**A Remarkable Collection**

When Alistair and Athena McAlpine moved to Apulia, British upper-class society was dumbfounded. What did this lord, once treasurer of Margaret Thatcher's Conservative Party, and his young wife, who had lived in such cosmopolitan cities as New York, see in this god-forsaken area down on the heel of Italy? But the answer was simple: the couple had found a perfect and private spot there, a place that had been shaped by different cultures like their own lives and was filled with colour and contrasts, a place whose raw beauty and magic aroused their urge to make discoveries. A former monastery became their home – and their treasure-house. Because Alistair had not just been politically active: a passionate collector, he had gathered over 14 tons of books and acquired thousands of examples of ethnic and folk art on his journeys round the world. With an unerring sense of style Athena shows fabrics from Morocco and Indonesia, works by Aborigines and Africans, painted glass from Kerala and parasols from Vietnam to best advantage and turns a diverse collection into a bohemian complete work of art. To be a guest of the McAlpines is to stay with friends and enjoy the relaxed Italian way of life at its very best. The food, too, matches the manners of the country: the Mediterranean meals have often been a reason for visitors to extend their stay. Not forgetting, of course, the charm of the hosts.

**Book to pack: "Casa Rossa" by Francesca Marciano.**

| | |
|---|---|
| **Convento di Santa Maria di Costantinopoli** | |
| Via Convento | |
| 73030 Marittima di Diso | |
| Italy | |
| Tel. +44 77 3636 2328 | |
| No fax; no website; no email address | |
| **Open from March to October** | |

| | |
|---|---|
| DIRECTIONS | 30 miles south of Lecce airport. |
| RATES | Price on request. |
| ROOMS | 9 rooms (without television, telephone and internet). |
| FOOD | On request exquisite Apulian dishes are served in the evening. |
| HISTORY | This former Franciscan monastery was used as a tobacco factory and even a scrap yard until the McAlpines gradually opened it to guests in 2004. |
| X-FACTOR | The owners' passion for collecting is evident even by the pool, which is surrounded by countless cacti. |

## Eine außergewöhnliche Sammlung

Als Alistair und Athena McAlpine nach Apulien zogen, verstand man in besseren britischen Kreisen die Welt nicht mehr. Was wollten der Lord, einst Schatzmeister von Margaret Thatcher, und seine junge Frau, die in Metropolen wie New York gelebt hatte, in einer gottverlassenen Gegend am Absatz des italienischen Stiefels? Dabei war die Antwort so einfach – die beiden hatten dort einen perfekten und privaten Platz gefunden, einen Ort, der wie ihr eigenes Leben von verschiedenen Kulturen geprägt worden und voller Farben und Kontraste war, der mit seiner rauen Schönheit und seiner Magie ihren Entdeckersinn weckte. Ein ehemaliges Kloster wurde zu ihrem Heim – und zum Hort ihrer Schätze. Denn Alistair war nicht nur Politiker gewesen: Als leidenschaftlicher Leser hatte er mehr als 14 Tonnen Bücher zusammengetragen und als Weltreisender Tausende Exponate von Stammes- und Volkskunst erstanden. Die Stoffe aus Marokko und Indonesien, die Arbeiten der Aborigines und Afrikaner, die Glasmalereien aus Kerala und die Schirme aus Vietnam setzt Athena absolut stilsicher in Szene und schafft aus dem Sammelsurium ein Gesamtkunstwerk der Boheme. Wer bei ihnen zu Gast ist, wohnt bei Freunden und genießt die italienische Lässigkeit in ihrer schönsten Form. Den guten Sitten des Landes entspricht auch das Essen: Die mediterranen Menüs waren schon mehrfach Grund dafür, dass Besucher ihren Aufenthalt verlängert haben – neben dem Charme der Gastgeber natürlich.
**Buchtipps:** »Otranto« von Roberto Cotroneo und »Casa Rossa« von Francesca Marciano.

## L'art de la collection

Lorsqu'Alistair et Athena McAlpine sont partis s'installer dans les Pouilles, la bonne société britannique n'en est pas revenue. Que cherchaient l'ancien trésorier de Margaret Thatcher et sa jeune femme dans un endroit perdu situé dans le talon de la botte italienne, eux qui avaient vécu dans des métropoles comme New York ? La réponse était simple pourtant – le couple a trouvé ici un paysage idéal et bien à lui, un endroit à son image marqué par différentes cultures et plein de couleurs et de contrastes, un lieu dont la beauté sauvage et la magie ont éveillé son instinct d'explorateur. Un ancien couvent est devenu leur foyer et l'écrin de leurs trésors. C'est que lord Alistair McAlpine ne s'est pas contenté de faire de la politique ; lecteur passionné, il a rassemblé plus de quatorze tonnes de livres et, voyageur infatigable, des milliers d'objets de l'art tribal et populaire. Avec une parfaite maîtrise stylistique, Athena met en scène des étoffes marocaines et indonésiennes, des travaux des Aborigènes et des Africains, des peintures sur verre du Kerala et des paravents du Vietnam, créant avec ces objets disparates une œuvre d'art totale tout à fait originale. Celui qui séjourne ici avec les McAlpine habite chez des amis et jouit de la nonchalance italienne sous sa forme la plus raffinée. La gastronomie est au rendez-vous : la cuisine méditerranéenne – et le charme des maîtres des lieux – en ont amené plus d'un à prolonger son séjour.
**Livres à emporter : « Le Soleil des Scorta »** de Laurent Gaudé et **« Casa Rossa »** de Francesca Marciano.

| | |
|---|---|
| ANREISE | 50 km südlich von Lecce gelegen. |
| PREISE | Preis auf Anfrage. |
| ZIMMER | 9 Zimmer (ohne Fernseher, Telefon und Internet). |
| KÜCHE | Auf Wunsch bekommt man auch abends feinste apulische Gerichte. |
| GESCHICHTE | Das einstige Franziskanerkloster wurde als Tabakfabrik und sogar Schrottplatz genutzt, ehe die McAlpines es 2004 nach und nach für Gäste öffneten. |
| X-FAKTOR | Selbst um den Pool herum zeigt sich die Sammelleidenschaft der Besitzer, hier stehen ungezählte Kakteen. |

| | |
|---|---|
| ACCÈS | À 50 km au sud de Lecce. |
| PRIX | Prix sur demande. |
| CHAMBRES | 9 chambres (sans téléviseur ni téléphone ou Internet). |
| RESTAURATION | Les plats les plus savoureux de la cuisine apulienne sont aussi servis le soir sur demande. |
| HISTOIRE | L'ancien couvent franciscain a servi d'usine de tabac et même de parc à ferraille avant que les McAlpine ne l'ouvrent progressivement pour leurs hôtes à partir de 2004. |
| LES « PLUS » | La piscine et ses innombrables cactus, une autre manifestation de la passion de la collection qui anime les propriétaires. |

# A Taste of Summer
Capofaro, Salina

# Capofaro, Salina

**A Taste of Summer**

The crowning glory of any dinner on Salina is Malvasia, a white wine that gleams golden-yellow in the glass, has a bouquet of raisins, candied fruit and lily of the valley at first, and then unfolds surprising, with delicate nuances of citronella and pepper. Only here, on the volcanic soil of the second-largest of the Aeolian Islands, are Malvasia grapes grown, then laid out to dry in the shade on straw mats before the pressing and fermentation takes place. The most elegant Malvasia wine is made by the Tasca D'Almerita family, a Sicilian dynasty whose wine estate has been one of the best in southern Italy for more than 150 years. The fitting place to enjoy this wine is the family's own Capofaro Resort, which lies at the edge of the vineyards and has a view far across the sea to Panarea and Stromboli. When the neighbouring islands shimmer pink and orange at sunset and the volcano spits glowing lava after dark, the sight is quite simply spectacular. The cottages, too, which are scattered around the estate and have flat roofs and terraces with blinds made of rushes in the Aeolian architectural tradition, boast panoramas fit for a painter's canvas. The interiors of the rooms do not even try to steal the show from the overwhelming beauty outdoors, but are white, minimalist and wonderfully soothing. The restaurant follows the same philosophy by concentrating on essentials, which is why it serves such excellent island dishes. The seafood in particular is a real treat for the taste buds – only the Malvasia tastes more of summer, sun and Salina.

**Book to pack: "Sicily" by Guy de Maupassant.**

**Capofaro Malvasia & Resort**

Tenuta Capofaro

Via Faro 3

98050 Salina

Italy

Tel. +39 090 9844 330 and 331

Fax +39 090 9844 339

info@capofaro.it

www.capofaro.it

**Open from the beginning of April to the end of September**

| | |
|---|---|
| DIRECTIONS | Guests who fly to Catania can ask the resort to book a transfer from the airport to Milazzo harbour. The fairy to Salina takes 90 min. |
| RATES | Rooms from 170 €, including breakfast. |
| ROOMS | 20 rooms in 7 cottages. |
| FOOD | The owners' cookery courses reveal the best Sicilian recipes. |
| HISTORY | Capofaro Resort takes its name from the cape and lighthouse that it overlooks. It was opened in 2004. |
| X-FACTOR | The beautiful pool makes up for the lack of a beach. |

## So schmeckt der Sommer

Er ist der krönende Abschluss eines jeden Dinners auf Salina: der Weißwein Malvasia, der goldgelb im Glas glänzt, erst nach Rosinen, kandierten Früchten und Maiglöckchen duftet und dann mit zarten Nuancen von Citronella sowie Pfeffer überrascht. Seine Trauben werden nur hier kultiviert – auf dem vulkanischen Boden der zweitgrößten Liparischen Insel – und im Schatten auf Strohmatten getrocknet, ehe sie gepresst und vergoren werden. Den elegantesten Malvasia keltert die Familie Tasca D'Almerita, eine sizilianische Dynastie, die seit mehr als 150 Jahren zu den besten Winzereien Süditaliens zählt. Ihren Wein genießt man am passendsten im familieneigenen Capofaro Resort, das am Rand der Rebhänge liegt und weit übers Meer bis nach Panarea sowie Stromboli blickt – wenn die Nachbarinseln bei Sonnenuntergang pinkorange schimmern und der Vulkan nach Einbruch der Dunkelheit glühende Lava spuckt, ist die Sicht schlicht spektakulär. Auch die Cottages, die sich auf dem Grundstück verteilen und nach äolischer Architekturtradition Flachdächer sowie Terrassen mit Schilfrohrmarkisen besitzen, eröffnen leinwandtaugliche Panoramen. Das Interieur der Zimmer versucht erst gar nicht, der überwältigenden Landschaft die Schau zu stehlen, sondern gibt sich ganz in Weiß, minimalistisch und wunderbar wohltuend. Derselben Philosophie folgt das Restaurant, das aufs Wesentliche reduziert ist und genau deshalb so gute Gerichte der Insel serviert. Vor allem die Meeresfrüchte sind echtes Gaumenglück – noch mehr nach Sommer, Sonne und Salina schmeckt nur der Malvasia.

**Buchtipp:** »Reise durch Sizilien« von Guy de Maupassant.

## Le goût de l'été

Le Malvasia delle Lipari est le couronnement de tout dîner à Salina : couleur jaune d'or, il embaume les fruits secs, les agrumes confits et le muguet avant de surprendre par ses nuances délicates de citronnelle et de poivre. Ses raisins blancs ne sont cultivés qu'ici, sur le sol volcanique de l'île, la deuxième de l'archipel des Eoliennes par sa superficie, et séchés à l'ombre sur des nattes de paille avant d'être pressés et de fermenter. Le malvoisie le plus élégant est produit par la famille Tasca D'Almerita, une dynastie sicilienne qui fait partie depuis plus d'un siècle et demi des meilleurs vignerons de l'Italie du Sud. Ils sont également propriétaires du Capofaro Resort, et la meilleure manière de déguster leur vin est de le faire dans cet hôtel situé au bord des versants plantés de vigne, et qui se dresse au-dessus de la mer avec vue sur Panarea et le Stromboli. Lorsque les îles voisines se teintent de rose orange au soleil couchant et que le volcan crache sa lave dans l'obscurité, la vue est tout simplement spectaculaire. Eparpillées sur le domaine, les petites maisons qui offrent des vues sublimes sur le paysage alentour sont typiquement éoliennes avec leurs toits plats et leurs terrasses dotées de stores en roseau. L'aménagement intérieur ne cherche pas à rivaliser avec l'extérieur extraordinaire et se contente de blanc minimaliste et merveilleusement bienfaisant. Le restaurant illustre la même philosophie en servant des plats de l'île réduits à l'essentiel, ce qui ne les rend que plus exquis. Les fruits de mer, surtout, sont un vrai délice – il n'y a que le malvoisie pour offrir plus encore le goût de l'été, du soleil et de l'île.

**Livre à emporter :** « En Sicile » de Guy de Maupassant.

| | | |
|---|---|---|
| ANREISE | Wer nach Catania fliegt, kann über das Resort einen Transfer vom Airport zum Hafen Milazzo buchen. Die Überfahrt nach Salina dauert 90 min. | |
| PREISE | Zimmer ab 170 €, inklusive Frühstück. | |
| ZIMMER | 20 Zimmer in 7 Cottages. | |
| KÜCHE | Die Besitzer verraten die besten sizilianischen Rezepte bei Kochkursen. | |
| GESCHICHTE | Das Capofaro Resort verdankt seinen Namen dem Kap mit Leuchtturm unterhalb der Anlage. Es wurde 2004 eröffnet. | |
| X-FAKTOR | Der schöne Pool macht den fehlenden Strand wett. | |

| | |
|---|---|
| ACCÈS | L'hôtel peut organiser un transfert de l'aéroport de Catane au port de Milazzo. Il faut compter 90 min de trajet jusqu'à Salina. |
| PRIX | Chambre à partir de 170 €, petit-déjeuner inclus. |
| CHAMBRES | 20 chambres dans 7 cottages. |
| RESTAURATION | Les propriétaires dévoilent les meilleures recettes siciliennes dans des cours de cuisine. |
| HISTOIRE | Le Capofaro Resort tient son nom du cap dominé par un phare. Il a ouvert ses portes en 2004. |
| LES « PLUS » | La piscine qui peut rivaliser avec une plage. |

# Where Italy is African
## Il Gattopardo, Isola di Lampedusa

# Il Gattopardo, Isola di Lampedusa

**Where Italy is African**

Sometimes a week without telephone, television and internet is just what you need – on an island set in the blue sea, a place that interests neither hotel chains nor jet-setters, where you can communicate with the locals using sign language because you hardly understand a word of their dialect, and where all you need to be perfectly content is a bed and a boat. Lampedusa is that kind of destination for time out from the daily grind. The largest of the Pelagian Islands, it has a raw beauty, with cliffs in the north and sandy bays in the south, where countless fish, dolphins and turtles swim in crystal-clear water. On land the flora and fauna betray African influences: Lampedusa is nearer to the Tunisian coast than to Sicily, and in geographical terms is part of Africa. To gain an authentic experience of the island and its atmosphere in the company of like-minded people, Il Gattopardo di Lampedusa is the right place to stay. The rustic-style rooms have the names of fish (Arganante and Scorfano, which have terraces with a sea view, are particularly charming rooms), and a wonderful leisure programme is included in the price: every day guests set off on a boat trip, during which the skipper prepares a delicious seafood lunch on board. In the evenings, too, fish dominates the menu – and when the other guests start to recall the day's events over a glass of wine, most of them have just one wish: if only they could spend some more time without telephone, television and internet!

**Book to pack: "The Leopard" by Giuseppe Tomasi di Lampedusa.**

| | |
|---|---|
| **Il Gattopardo di Lampedusa**<br>Via Beta 6<br>Contrada Cala Creta<br>92010 Lampedusa<br>Italy<br>Tel. information +39 0922 970 051<br>Tel. booking +39 011 818 5211 (tour operator:<br>Equinoxe)<br>equinoxe@equinoxe.it<br>www.gattopardodilampedusa.it<br>**Open from the end of May to the end of October** | **DIRECTIONS** Lampedusa lies between Sicily and Tunisia. The easiest way to reach the island is to fly from Palermo (45 min) or Catania (70 min).<br><br>**RATES** Weekend package 1,250 € per person in a double room (2,100 € for single occupancy), including full board, boat trips and rental car. No children under the age of 16.<br><br>**ROOMS** 14 rooms.<br><br>**FOOD** For dinner there is a set several-course meal that changes daily.<br><br>**HISTORY** The hotel was modeled after the French "maison d'hôtes".<br><br>**X-FACTOR** A visit to the idyllic neighbouring island of Linosa. |

## Wo Italien afrikanisch wird

Manchmal braucht man einfach eine Woche ohne Telefon, Fernseher und Internet. Auf einer Insel im Blauen, die für Hotelketten genauso uninteressant ist wie für Jetsetter, wo man sich mit den Einheimischen mit Händen und Füßen unterhält, weil man ihren Dialekt kaum versteht, und wo ein Bett und ein Boot genügen, um das Glück perfekt zu machen. Lampedusa ist solch ein Ziel für eine Auszeit vom Alltag. Die größte der drei Pelagischen Inseln besitzt eine raue Schönheit mit Steilklippen im Norden und Sandbuchten im Süden, vor denen in kristallklarem Wasser ungezählte Fische, Delfine sowie Schildkröten schwimmen. An Land sind Flora und Fauna afrikanisch angehaucht – Lampedusa liegt der tunesischen Küste näher als der sizilianischen und gehört geografisch bereits zu Afrika. Wer das Ambiente der Insel authentisch und in Gesellschaft Gleichgesinnter erleben möchte, ist im Gattopardo di Lampedusa an der richtigen Adresse. Hier sind die rustikalen Zimmer nach Fischen benannt (besonders charmant sind die Räume »Arganante« und »Scorfano«, die Terrassen mit Meerblick besitzen), und im Preis inbegriffen ist ein herrliches Freizeitprogramm: Jeden Tag legen die Gäste zu einem Bootsausflug ab, bei dem der Skipper an Bord das köstlichste Mittagessen aus Meeresfrüchten zubereitet. Auch abends bestimmt Fisch die Karte – und wenn die Mitbewohner auf Zeit bei einem Glas Wein das Erlebte Revue passieren lassen, haben die meisten nur einen Wunsch: Könnte die Zeit ohne Telefon, Fernseher und Internet doch nur länger dauern!

**Buchtipp: »Der Leopard« von Giuseppe Tomasi di Lampedusa.**

## Là où l'Italie devient africaine

On a parfois besoin de passer une semaine sans téléphone, sans télévision et sans Internet. Sur une île aussi peu intéressante pour les chaînes hôtelières que pour la jet-set, dans un endroit où l'on parle avec ses mains aux gens parce qu'on ne comprend pas leur langue, et où un lit et un bateau suffisent à rendre heureux. Lampedusa est l'une de ces destinations. La plus vaste des îles Pélages possède une beauté rude avec des falaises abruptes au nord et des baies de sable au sud, dans lesquelles d'innombrables poissons, des dauphins et des tortues nagent dans l'eau limpide. Sa flore et sa faune terrestre sont similaires à celles de l'Afrique du Nord, Lampedusa est en effet plus proche de la côte tunisienne que de la Sicile et fait partie géographiquement de l'Afrique. Celui qui veut goûter une atmosphère authentique en compagnie de gens partageant les mêmes idées est à la bonne adresse au Il Gattopardo di Lampedusa. Ici, les chambres rustiques portent des noms de poisson (« Arganante » et « Scorfano » qui possèdent des terrasses avec vue sur la mer sont particulièrement charmantes) et un magnifique programme d'activités est compris dans le séjour : les hôtes font tous les jours une excursion en bateau et, le midi, le skipper leur offre de délicieux fruits de mer préparés par ses soins. Le soir aussi, le poisson est à l'honneur, et les heureux vacanciers réfléchissent à ce qu'ils ont fait pendant la journée en dégustant un verre de vin. La plupart n'ont qu'un désir : s'il pouvait seulement durer, ce temps sans téléphone, sans télévision et sans Internet.

**Livre à emporter : « Le Guépard » de Giuseppe Tomasi di Lampedusa.**

| ANREISE | Lampedusa liegt zwischen Sizilien und Tunesien. Am besten ist die Insel per Flugzeug von Palermo (45 min) oder Catania (70 min) zu erreichen. |
|---|---|
| PREISE | Wochenpauschale ab 1.250 € pro Person im Doppelzimmer (2.100 € bei Einzelnutzung), inklusive Vollpension, Boots-touren und Mietwagen. Kinder werden erst ab 16 Jahren willkommen geheißen. |
| ZIMMER | 14 Zimmer. |
| KÜCHE | Zum Dinner gibt es ein festes Menü, das täglich wechselt. |
| GESCHICHTE | Das Hotel wurde nach dem Vorbild der französischen »maison d'hôtes« gestaltet. |
| X-FAKTOR | Ein Besuch der idyllischen Nachbarinsel Linosa. |

| ACCÈS | L'île est située entre la Sicile et la Tunisie. On peut l'atteindre par avion de Palerme (45 min) ou de Catane (70 min). |
|---|---|
| PRIX | Forfait hebdomadaire à partir de 1250 € par personne en chambre double (2100 € si vous l'utilisez seul), pension complète, excursions en bateau et voitures de louage. Les enfants ne sont accueillis qu'à partir de 16 ans. |
| CHAMBRES | 14 chambres. |
| RESTAURATION | Le menu du dîner change tous les jours. |
| HISTOIRE | L'hôtel a été aménagé sur le modèle de la maison d'hôtes française. |
| LES « PLUS » | La visite de Linosa, l'île voisine au paysage idyllique. |

# Photo Credits | Fotonachweis
# Crédits photographiques

© 2010 TASCHEN GmbH
Hohenzollernring 53, D-50672 Köln
www.taschen.com

To stay informed about upcoming TASCHEN titles, please request our magazine at www.taschen.com/magazine or write to TASCHEN, Hohenzollernring 53, D-50672 Cologne, Germany; contact@taschen.com; Fax: +49-221-254919. We will be happy to send you a free copy of our magazine, which is filled with information about all of our books.

| | |
|---|---|
| COMPILED, EDITED AND LAYOUT: | Angelika Taschen, Berlin |
| PROJECT COORDINATOR: | Angela Roberts, Cologne |
| TEXTS: | Christiane Reiter, Hamburg |
| FRENCH TRANSLATION: | Michèle Schreyer, Cologne |
| ENGLISH TRANSLATION: | John Sykes, Cologne |
| DESIGN: | Lambert und Lambert, Düsseldorf |
| LITHOGRAPH MANAGER: | Thomas Grell, Cologne |
| PRINTED IN | China |
| ISBN | 978-3-8365-1581-8 |